Songs of the Saints from the Adi Granth

Songs of the Saints from the Adi Granth

Translation and Introduction
by Nirmal Dass

State University of New York Press

Published by
State University of New York Press, Albany

Printed in the United States of America

For information, address State University of New York Press, 90 State Street, Suite 700, Albany, NY 12207

Production by Diane Ganeles
Marketing by Fran Keneston

Cover Photo: Shows a *virahini nayaka* (pining woman), symbolic of the soul yearning for God (Kishangarh School, mid-18th century). From the translator's private collection.

Library of Congress Cataloging-in-Publication Data

Adi-Granth. English. Selections.
Songs of the saints from the Adi Granth / translation and introduction, Nirmal Dass.
p. cm.
Translated from Hindi.
Includes bibliographical references and index.
ISBN 0-7914-4683-2 (acid free) — ISBN 0-7914-4684-0 (pb : acid free)
1. Sikh hymns, English. I. Dass, Nirmal, 1962–

BL2017.4.A4 D37 2000
294.6′82—dc21

99-054419

10 9 8 7 6 5 4 3 2 1

un du corps comme du coeur

CONTENTS

PREFACE

The saints, whose works are translated in this volume, constitute a unique component in The Adi Granth, the Sikh Scripture. Their works as preserved in this holy book greatly enrich Sikh tradition and piety whose history stretches back to the twelfth century. As is often the case with Indian hagiography, we know very little about the lives of these saints, and even dates are no more than guesswork. To translate their writings has meant embarking on a journey through the entire breadth of north Indian history and culture, which sees the past as not something foreign, but as an ever-present reality that informs and grounds each and every utterance. The songs of these saints are also the earliest—and often the only—recensions that we possess.

This translation brings together in one volume the songs and proverbs (slokas) of the saints of The Adi Granth. The key figure missing is Kabir, whose work I have translated separately in *Songs of Kabir from the Adi Granth* (Albany: State University of New York Press, 1991; Delhi, India: Sri Satguru Publications, 1992). Although previous translations of some of these saints exist, there has never been an attempt to bring all of them into one volume.

My primary source has been *Adi Guru Granth Sahib Ji*, ed. *Gyani Mohindar Singh "Ratan"* (Amritsar, India: Bhai Chatar Singh Jivan Singh Pustakanvale, n.d.); also indispensable was Kahan Singh Nabha's *Mahan Kosh* (Patiala, India: Bhasha Vibhag, 1926).

INTRODUCTION

The songs of the Hindu and Muslim saints (sants) that are translated in this volume are an integral part of Sikh piety and Scripture. The youngest religion of India had its inception with the teachings of Guru Nanak (1469–1539), in the Panjab.

In 1604–5, the fifth Sikh guru, Arjan Dev (1563–1606), gave the community its Scripture, The Adi Granth (The primal book), which was an anthology containing the standardized and codified songs (bani) of the four previous gurus (plus Guru Arjan Dev's own compositions), and the songs of fifteen pre-Nanak saints. Guru Arjan Dev sought to give his community a compilation that would rival The Rig Veda of the Hindus.[1]

Many of these saints flourished well before Guru Nanak, but their teachings expounded beliefs that were of paramount importance to Sikhism itself. Thus by apposing the saints with the songs of the gurus, Arjan placed the tenets of the new faith within a religious context that stretched back to the twelfth century, if not earlier. Consequently, Guru Arjan Dev not only enriched Sikh piety by historically contextualizing it, but more importantly he gave it a prehistory. Therefore, the fifteen saints are not merely an adjunct to The Adi Granth, nor are they marginal to the teachings of the gurus; rather they are the intertextual ground from which Sikh piety itself springs—for prehistory implies continuity. In brief, the words of the gurus complete the utterances of the various saints: the old flows into the new, and the new encompasses the old; both receive and perfect each other.

Radical Indian religiosity has always been liminal: it knows no boundaries; it questions everything; it freely appropriates names, concepts, and places them into new contexts; it forever ruptures texts—in order to disseminate the Word (shabad), which alone can house the Divine. It is within this liminality that Sikhism itself inscribes its mark by transplanting/translating previous methods of naming the Divine in northern India within the confines of its own creed. It is instructive to briefly examine the various traditions from which Sikhism garners its own identity.

Chief among these traditions is santism,[2] which is a constitutive, polysemic approach to the Divine, where the One is seen in the many, and the many give way to the One. The saints of The Adi Granth are firmly rooted in this belief, and they deny all canonized versions of the Divine—for them anything visible and external can only be a manifestation—which by its very nature is merely a paraphrase, a metaphor for the Divine. Thus there is no need for ritual, idol-worship, scriptural authority, Brahminism, divine incarnations (sagun), or castes, since it is not through these that the Divine is realized. Rather the object of devotion for these saints is the Primal Essence, the Being of beings, the Godhead who is internal, without form, unchanging, without attributes (nirgun), unincarnated: "He is unseen / like fragrance in a flower"(Namdeva, *Raga Gujri* 2, p. 33). The externality of systems must give way to the internality of personal experience (parcha): God can only be experienced; He cannot be known through religious systems, rituals, or spiritual discipline.[3]

The process of apperceiving the Divine begins with the realization that since the Divine is diffused in all things, it is therefore present in each individual: "In all things / exists the Lord, / assuming countless shapes; / in each pore he plays and sports. . . . He is nearer than my hand" (Ravi Dass, *Raga Sorath* 1, p. 100).

This immediately accessible God, however, is also infinitely distant; He is Parbrahma (beyond Brahma), the God beyond all gods who sits in silence, the ground of all that is—yet distinct Himself: "Primal, / All-pervasive, / Unrivaled, / Unchanging, / First Mover, / Hoard of virtue. / All-powerful, / Beyond creation, / Incomprehensible, / Forever present" (Jayadeva, *Raga Gujri*, p. 132). All other gods are His creation, His shadow; the sant adores and loves not the shadow, but He who casts it. However, the Creator of many forms is Himself without form (rupa); He is all forms and none. Thus He can only be known through His Name (nam). The sant meditates upon, and loves, this Name.[4]

The experience of the Divine is brought home by the guru, the essential component in the salvific process of the individual soul. The guru is at the juncture of the crossing of the human and the Divine, at the articulation of the chiasmus where God and human beings intersect. It is there that the position of the guru is marked: "Man becomes god in an instant, / when the guru gives him wisdom" (Namdeva, *Raga Gaund* 3, p. 47).

This articulation is the confluence and the dehiscence of the Divine within humanity. Therefore, the guru is not only a teacher, but an accomplished person himself in that he has already acquired God and arrived at the perfected state (param pada) wherein he can merge with the Creator of all things. But while he is in the world, he is instrumental in helping others to achieve perfection.[5] His instruction (bani) and his grace (parshad) instill illumination whereby the ignorant soul discovers the Divine within itself. The site where this event occurs is within the human mind (often called the Tenth Door), where the growth, maturation, and dehiscence of the Divine takes place; and only the guru can mark this spot, the X, where the Divine can burst open like a mature pod and disseminate Itself. The guru is God's channel; God bestows on him his bani and parshad—and he bestows on others what he himself has received.

Housed within the bani is the Word (shabad)—the identity, the mark of God Himself. The Johannine principle of the logos is discernible here—the Word was (and is) God. The guru mediates the confluence of the soul with God. This union (vismad) produces supreme bliss (param-ananda), which is beyond the reach of language, just as the Word lies outside of all words, beyond language itself: "The tale cannot be told, / so why speak further? / You are what You are. / What metaphor / can I possibly use / to describe You?"(Ravi Dass, *Raga Bilaval* 1, p. 113).

The guru, then, is the pointer to the silent abode of God, which is the true destination of all souls: "What are the manifestations / of Dev's abode? / There, / resounds the Word unspoken. / There, / neither moon nor sun, / air nor water exist" (Beni, *Raga Ramkali*, p. 153).

Given this proximity of the Divine, there is no longer any real need for traditional methods of religiosity: Scriptures, idols, rituals, and castes are unimportant. With the negation of official Hindu practice, the traditional liturgical language, Sanskrit, is also abandoned in favor of the vernacular.[6] Further, the duties of house and home (grihasti) are expounded since renunciation of the world (sanyas) is deemed futile. The emphasis here is not on pursuing salvation in a solitary fashion, but rather to engage actively in the flow and flux of the world in order to help others gain salvation. Thus it is not surprising that the sants continued to practice their traditional occupations, while they propagated their beliefs: Sain remained a barber, Ravi Dass a cobbler, Namdeva a calico-printer, Dhanna a farmer.

Within Santism, another strand is discernible, namely, Nathism, or the creed of the Yogis who follow the teachings of Gorakh Datta (ca. twelfth century). Nathism expounded salvation through the rigors of Yoga and asceticism, along with various Tantric and Buddhist practices.[7] The Naths were adept at hatha-yoga; this allowed them to physically experience union (samadhi) with the Divine.[8] The Naths denied scriptural and religious authority and maintained that the Divine was in-dwelling. Once the union between the Divine and the soul took place, the Yogi became a man-god, who commanded supernatural powers and even had the gods at his beck and call. Although the sants themselves rejected the practice of Yoga as a spiritual vehicle, they nevertheless borrowed the Naths' vast Yogic grammar and vocabulary, in their efforts to describe the confluence of the Divine with the human. Thus it is that Yogic tropes are often deployed within the songs contained in The Adi Granth.

Sikhism certainly drew upon the attitudes and postulates of the sants, yet it is too easy to conclude from this context a similitude to preexisting structures—for prehistory cannot be history of the present. Thus claims that bind Sikhism to specific anterior systems and precepts must be carefully examined. It is of course certain that Santism greatly influenced Sikh doctrine; however it would be a mistake to therefore determine that Sikhism itself is systematized or clarified Santism.[9] But here let us briefly turn aside from the prehistory and examine the specific history of Sikhism, in order to fully comprehend the difference between these two systems of belief.

The development of Sikhism was the result of three particular stages that delimited the personality of the new faith.[10]

First, it was Guru Nanak who established the doctrinal, ethical, and structural ground. He stressed the unity that exists between one human being and another, and between a human being and the Divine. This unity was the source of all ethical conduct: by recognizing that the Divine was present in all, the individual accepted the equality of all. Thus pantheism was extended to include social responsibility. Guru Nanak put in place essential binaries that summarized his teachings as well as those of the sants before him. For example, his theology concedes that there is a perpetual coalescence of the Divine and the human, the guru and the disciple, past action (karma) and present status, society and piety, freedom and enslavement, transience (maya) and permanence, sound (nada) and nonsound (anahata), transmigration and salvation (moksha), worldly love (lobh) and devotion (bhakti), and physicality (kirat) and spirituality. The sum of these binaries is a harmony and balance of three things: good action, knowledge, and divine love. Good action improved the physical body (which was adjudged a holy temple wherein the Divine itself resided), and engendered charity. Knowledge purified the mind, for it was the sole human capability that allowed cognition of the in-dwelling God. And divine love elutriated the soul from the dross of the mundane and thereby kindled a yearning for God. On the structural level, Guru Nanak established a tripartite system of service that reflected this inner balance. First, there was the pangat or the langar, the communal kitchen where everyone worked and ate without discrimination. This dislodged caste barriers,[11] and freed the individual from received prejudices. Second, he founded the sangat (congregation) which participated in, and expounded, divine knowledge through the bani (the guru's word) and meditation. Third, he established the dharamsala (religious hall) which provided for the communal and spiritual needs of the new fellowship where the individual could actively participate in service to God and to humanity. At the same time, Guru Nanak counterchecked the authority of Hindu Scriptures, and in their place espoused the singing of hymns that he, or other sants, had composed.

The second stage is associated with Guru Arjan Dev in that he provided the Sikhs with their own Scripture in the body of The Adi Granth, which he ceremoniously installed in the Golden Temple (the *Harimandir*, "Temple of the Lord") at Amritsar. By way of this formality he made visible the veneration of the Word (shabad) as contained in the words of the gurus and sants (the bani). The Adi Granth also differentiated between the Sikhs and the Hindus (a distinction never previously established), thus engendering a stronger sense of community. At the same time, Guru Arjan instituted the practice of tithing (daswandh), the revenue from which he used to construct various buildings and shrines. He also became the first Sikh martyr, who was sentenced to a torturous execution by the emperor Jahangir in 1606 for his role in assisting the fleeing prince Khusrau.[12] Guru Arjan's execution shifted the focus from the pure pursuit of peace to self-preservation for the Sikhs. Therefore, Arjan's son, Har Gobind, who became the sixth guru, began to militarize the community—a strategy that would culminate in the work of Gobind Singh, the tenth and last Sikh guru.[13]

The final stage in Sikhism is associated with Guru Gobind Singh (1666–1708). It was he who created and defined the Khalsa (the pure), a sect of warrior-saints within the larger body of Sikhism, who pledged to protect the innocent, to fight injustice, to defend the weak, and to uphold truth and righteousness. This enmeshing of the sword with saintliness further served to distinguish the Sikhs from their Hindu compatriots. For most of his life, Guru Gobind Singh fought the oppression of the Mughal rulers; his own father Tegh Bahadur (1622–75), the ninth Sikh guru, was executed by the zealot emperor Aurangzeb.[14] During his struggles with the Mughal authorities, Gobind Singh lost his four sons and was hounded out of the Panjab.[15] He took up abode at Nander in Haiderabad; one year later, he was fatally stabbed by an Afghan retainer. Before he died, Gobind Singh proclaimed The Adi Granth as the living guru, thus bringing to an end the line of human gurus that had ruled the Sikh community from the time of Guru Nanak.[16]

It is this history of Sikhism that is apposed to its prehistory; upon comparison, the differences between the two are pronounced. Santism never rose beyond its spirit of protest. As a critique of official Hinduism it worked well; but as its replacement, Santism failed since it could not sufficiently separate itself from Hinduism. Sikhism, on the other hand, was never successfully assimilated, and remained a distinct system of belief: one that continually sought to segregate itself from other faiths and creeds. Thus Sikhism went beyond mere criticism—it offered an alternative. Consequently, prehistory was used as a critique of current religious systems and canons, while the work of the gurus itself provided a newer piety, a "better" way as it were: one that always sought to be practical and responsible, where an individual could be pious and could function effectively in the affairs of the world.

To say that Sikhism is systematized Santism is to allow similarities to determine identity, for definition is always and only about identity. However, we must allow for the play of difference. We must see the prehistory of Sikhism, as housed in the work of the pre-Nanak saints, as intertextual contexts embedded within the body of The Adi Granth. The hymns (bani) of the gurus merge and become separated from these intertextualities, and it is through these contexts that Sikhism arrives at a specificity, an identity. The Adi Granth is a polyvalent fabric and text(ure) that weaves the perceptions of many saints into one theology. The Adi Granth as Scripture can only determine itself because of, and through, other texts contained within it—for it is itself always an intertext.

In fact, the heuristic force being asserted in The Adi Granth is intertextuality; it is the very ground of the Scripture's prehistory. The Adi Granth is the primal book that paradoxically knows no beginning, middle, or end; each of its songs and hymns comes into being through, and because of, an interplay with prehistory: ". . . [a]

text is a relational event, and not a substance to be analyzed."[17] The fabric has many threads, for no text is the absolute origin of another text, nor is one text the parent of all other texts. Thus Sikhism is not refashioned Santism, nor is it a harmonization of Hinduism and Islam. And we learn this fact from the faith's prehistory. Sikhism is an inscription of codependent relationships, each one presupposing and determining the other; and its Scripture houses the unending play and interplay of texts and intertexts: "Wave upon water, / water within wave: / The difference is only / in our speaking and hearing" (Namdeva, *Raga Sarang* 2, p. 75). The rhythm itself of interplay is endless; similarity cannot exist without difference: what is wave and what is water, though both contain a similitude to the other? Texts know no boundaries; they cross over; they interweave; the endless flux "within the . . . text should not be identified with an organic process of maturation or a hermeneutic process of deepening, but rather with a serial movement of dislocations, overlappings, and variations."[18] The Adi Granth presents us with a perpetual fable of words: they rise and pass; the text brings this rising and passing into being, and the book itself holds the texture, the weave of this primal play (lila)—mirrored so minutely in the interplay between the human and the Divine, between the Creator and His creation, between life and death. This dynamic the sants and the gurus understand well, for we too rise and pass—brought into being—and life itself holds the texture of our allotted span of years.

Our alignment, therefore, should not be to origins and originality, but the polysemic significations of intertextuality, which assures us that all writing is rewriting and reinscription; indeed writing is the perpetual play (lila) of difference, which points to the relativity of all that is—thus is water, wave, and wave, water. Intertextuality and interrelativity, therefore, constitute the Spielraum (lila) of the Divine: "If You are the lamp, / then I am the wick. / If You are the shrine, / then I am the pilgrim" (Ravi Dass, *Raga Sorath* 5, p. 103). Things come and go through the interplay of universal forces of life and death; nothing comes into being by its own self. Thus it is that writing (the lila of difference) is not only semiosis, but it is also kenosis—for it empties the self of itself—and this is moksha, salvation, the release of the self from the self: ". . . no one belongs to anyone: / like a tree is home to many birds" (Namdeva, *Raga Ramkali* 3, p. 53).

The force of intertextuality impels us to realize that origination is always codependent; nothing bears full autonomy. Even the omniscience and omnipotence of the Divine is marked thus: ". . . I am the Life of the world; / yet My slave is My life" (Namdeva, *Raga Sarang* 3, p. 75). In the theology of The Adi Granth, codependence and intertextuality, is everything: "The one thread strings / innumerable beads— . . . River and waves, / foam and bubbles / have all their being / within water itself. / This play of things / is the sport [lila] of Parbhama. / The One cannot be thought / different from the other" (Namdeva, *Raga Asa* 1, p. 29).

Prehistory is then intertext and context. And such is the relationship between the songs of the saints and the Sikh gurus in The Adi Granth, for prehistory provides a specific and specified ground upon which Sikh piety marks its being. Prehistory unwinds the constitutive threads, the semes, which Sikhism twines and weaves into a polysemic fabric all its own.

Concern for the prehistory of Sikh tenets, however, has antecedents earlier than Guru Arjan Dev.[19] When The Adi Granth was compiled, it served two purposes. First, it canonized the works of the previous four gurus. Second, it negated various spurious songs and proverbs attributed to past gurus by the factions hostile to Arjan's guruship.[20] The canonized version drew its structure from the collection put together by the third guru, Amar Dass (1479–1574) which appeared in two volumes. This collection, known as the *Goindval Pothis* (The Goindval books), consisted of the songs of Guru Nanak, Guru Angad (1504–53), and Guru Amar Dass. More importantly for us, the *Pothis* included the works of Kabir, Namdeva, Trilochan, Sain, Ravi Dass, and Jayadeva. Thus, a careful preservation of the prehistory of the new faith is already evident in the earliest attempts at canonization. Although it is difficult to say exactly when this apposition of the *Bani* of the saints and the gurus occurred, we can note that the songs of Guru Nanak show pronounced similarities with some songs of Kabir, Namdeva, Ravi Dass, and Sheikh Farid.

It can be said that Guru Arjan Dev expanded the process begun by Guru Amar Dass in that he collected the complete works of the previous four gurus, including the hymns of his father Guru Ram Dass (1534–81), then included his own, and expanded the number of saints to be included in his anthology, in order to show the diversity from which Sikhism drew its doctrine. Arjan arranged these songs according to thirty-one musical measures (ragas) which facilitated their performance; thus it is that devotional hymns are the key component in Sikh worship. Later, Guru Gobind Singh added the songs of his father, Guru Tegh Bahadur to the body of The Adi Granth.[21]

As Scripture, The Adi Granth propounds ethical and spiritual precepts that can be summarized thus: the need to improve the human condition by inculcating responsibility for the individual within society—not apart from it, and the exigency of realizing that salvation is the loss of self through union with the Divine. In other words, the emphasis is on recognizing the inherent unity between humanity, society, and spirituality: all things participate in each other and in God. Thus the text is a trope for being and Being in The Adi Granth.

Structurally, The Adi Granth contains the following divisions: (1) Japji (a morning prayer by Guru Nanak); (2) Rahiras Sahib (an evening prayer in two ragas by Guru Nanak, Guru Ram Dass, and Guru Arjan Dev); (3) Sohila (a night prayer in four ragas by Guru Nanak, Guru Ram Dass, and Guru Arjan Dev); (4) Ragas (songs in thirty-one ragas by the gurus and saints); (5) Slokas and Swayyas (miscellaneous proverbs of the gurus and saints, along with paeans by court poets in the employ of various gurus); and (6) Ragamala (a metric list of ragas).

Given that the bulk of the songs of the saints is found in the Raga section of The Adi Granth, it is worthwhile to briefly examine the musical system deployed by Guru Arjan Dev as an organizational principle and structuring device in his anthology.

This classification by way of ragas is evident in other collections of Indian religious verse, such as Jayadeva's *Gita Govinda*. The tradition itself of combining music and religious verse goes back to *The Rig Veda* that exploits an elaborate scheme of meters and chant styles in order to organize the various hymns.[22] Here it is important to recall that Guru Arjan Dev is also assembling a new Veda for his community—one that does not praise the various gods, but rather the Supreme God who is the Creator of these gods. And here is a crucial point: Guru Arjan Dev is intentionally writing a Scripture and thereby rewriting Hinduism. Just as *The Rig Veda* has its ten mandalas, so The Adi Granth deploys thirty-one ragas. And it is within the notational cycle of these musical measures that the bulk of the teaching (bani) is contained: "The jewel-like *Ragas*, with their fairy wives and families, came to sing the *Shabad*" (Guru Amar Dass, *The Anand Sahib*).

Legend has it that when Guru Arjan Dev sat down to compose and compile The Adi Granth, by the waters of Ramsar (The pool of God), in Amritsar, all the ragas (which have long been personified in Indian tradition as men with wives [raginis] and sons [putras]) came to the guru and pleaded with him to set things in order, for their correct usage and performance was being neglected and their "families" were being garbled or forgotten. In acquiescence, the legend continues, Guru Arjan Dev instituted the ragas as essential components in his new *Granth*—thus marrying sacred word with music.

This legend leads us directly into the very heart of Indian aesthetics. A raga is a musical measure, a structure, which spawns and determines various tunes. Thus it is always greater than the sum of its part, for it is a syntagmatic arrangement that gives birth to various—and unending—paradigmatic performances. As a syntagma, a raga perpetually engenders interplay with its many paradigms. Therefore, it is not surprising that Guru Arjan Dev chooses the *raga* as a synthesizing device—since his *Granth* also unceasingly engages in interplay with various binaries, countless texts.

Raga literally means "color" and as such is associated with a particular emotion (rasa), a specific time of day or night, a season of the year. Upon performance, this "color," this range of associative properties, undulates through the audience, imbuing—staining—each listener.

According to Indian musical theory, the shape of music is marked by the chiasmus, the intersection of binaries, the interplay of opposites—in that each note carries within it both nada (sound) and anahat (sound that is yet to be struck; silence in fact). Here again, we are in the realm of the syntagmatic (anahat) and the paradigmatic (nada), for music, like The Adi Granth, is that place, that site, where silence and sound cross. Since silence is the sphere of the Divine and sound the realm of humanity, it can also be said that music marks the crossing, the play (lila), of the human and the Divine. In order to produce sound, there must first be the potential for that sound—a nothingness (sunya) that yields the ground, the vacuum, which sound can fill, just as humanity is the ground of the Divine, and vice versa, wherein each can gain its full potential. Thus the interplay continues: thing and no-thing, the visible and the invisible, human and God, nada and anahat—merge and blend into each other in order to produce that melic intertexuality which is the vocalized shape of a raga, which is the constituted form of The Adi Granth, which is the union of a soul and God.

Indian aesthetics recognizes ten emotions (rasas) that abound in literature, drama, dance, painting, and music: the erotic, the comic, the pathetic, the violent, the heroic, the horrific, the hateful, the wondrous, the devotional, and the tranquil. The dominant rasas of The Adi Granth, according to the thirty-one ragas, are the devotional and the erotic: the individual soul is the pining woman who yearns for union with her beloved (God); such emotion is the result of extreme devotion, since the soul does not abandon its beloved and seek fulfillment in other "lovers." The time of performance covers the entire twenty-four hours—thus devotion and desire are presented as immutable conditions of the human soul.

These two rasas find contiguity with the songs of the saints as well. They continually speak of the in-dwelling God who sets in motion the entire play (lila) of love. And here is the key to these songs that unlocks their "secret" wisdom: it is through love that the divine Beloved comes to dwell in each life-form; it is through love that the individual seeks Him out; it is through love that the soul surrenders to the World Soul, completely losing its identity, achieving full and everlasting union. And what is the nature of this love? It is "Like a lustful woman smitten by a stranger, / like the greedy forever craving money, / like a woman to a lecherous man" (Namdeva, *Raga Bhairo* 7, p. 63).

But this union of opposites (the human and the Divine) is also an act that transcends syntactic and linguistic classifications—because it is an event (*parcha*), outside language, fully free of delimitation—just as the Divine is alien to language altogether; and what it touches is itself transfigured, translated into the indescribable, into that primal state (*param-pada*) where words decay, and meaning itself slips outside of language: ". . . [He] cannot be described, / He is everywhere, in everything. / Just as a mute when he drinks the sweetest nectar / cannot describe what he is tasting" (Namdeva, *Raga Sorath* 2, p. 36).

What then is the realm of the Divine? According to these saints, it is precisely nothingness, silence (sunya); it is a void that cannot and will not be filled. Yet paradoxically—and the Divine is a paradox—this emptiness is a nothingness that is completely filled: a precise equilibrium of "out-flow" and "in-flow": "The one thread strings / innumerable beads" (Namdeva, *Raga Asa* 1, p. 29). It was emptiness first that filled itself in order to make itself manifest: "First God appeared. . . . From That into this" (Namdeva, *Raga Dhanashri* 4, p. 39). Within the paradox of opposites—"This (the Divine) and "that" (all creation)—lies the play of being: "The blossom vanishes / so that fruit may appear" (Ravi Dass, *Raga Bhairo*, p. 122).

The trope of disappearance that these saints so often use has certainly been effective as far as biographical details are concerned. What we know about the lives of these saints is at best superficial and legendary. But a linear historical record is not really the issue. What we have before us demonstrates perfectly the union with the Divine that was the chief end for these saints—it is the meeting of history with ahistory, where linearity is subsumed by circularity, where sound again becomes silence, and where the void empties so that it may be filled. This union is a transhistorical event, valid for all time. Therefore to demand historical precision from the lives of these saints, and from Indian hagiography in general, is to miss the subtlety of the tradition.

The lives of these saints depend not upon our knowledge of who they were, where they lived, and what kind of characters they had. Rather their lives are *exempla*, paradigmatic representations of the syntagmatic Divine, which intersects and crosses the flow of human birth. The saints as people show the strength of the whole, rather than the uniqueness of the individual member.[23]

Consequently, history in Indian hagiography is not factual accountability but a narrativization, a plethora of stories which, when gathered, constitute not a life but a construction of the lila between "this" and "that." In a fragment, Empedocles tells us, "They were before and will continue being as they now are, and, I think, endless time will never be void of these two."[24] For our purposes, we can construe "these two" as opposites that come into play: the Divine that lies buried deep within humanity, the paradox of the mutable and the immutable; or as Meister Eckhardt states: "It is not outside, it is within; wholly within."[25] Here we have ontological intertextuality itself: Being and beings must both intersect in order to exist—for there cannot be Silence without sound—"You and I, / I and You— / how are we different? / Only in the sense / that gold / differs from the bracelet, / and water / differs from the wave" (Ravi Dass, *Sri Raga*, p. 86).

Thus the Divine needs humanity to complete itself, and humanity needs the Divine to perfect itself. This codependence is the nub of the songs of the saints translated in this volume; their verses are descriptions of the drama of the soul: its divine origin, its exile in the world, its desire to return to its true source and counterpart, and its final union with God. Once this union takes place, the soul becomes God, each filling the void of the other, and deriving "a simple unity, without any mode, without time and space, without before or after, without desire or possession, without light or darkness . . . a perpetual now. . . ."[26] This is the beginning and end of all things, the play of creation and destruction; into this sunya the yearning soul plunges and disappears into God: "There, /

resounds the Word unspoken" (Beni, *Raga Ramkali*, p. 153).

Any attempt at translating songs from The Adi Granth certainly involves working not with one language, but several, along with dialectical differences. The languages used by the saints range from Sanskrit; regional Prakrits; western, eastern and southern Apabhramsa; and Sahaskrit. More particularly, we find sant-bhasha, Marathi, Old Hindi, central and Lehndi Panjabi, Sindhi, and Persian. There are also many dialects deployed, such as, Purbi, Marwari, Bangru, Dakhni, Malwai, and Avadhi. This richness points to the fact that translation is not done in a vacuum—there is no neutral way to translate because words trail with them their own universe comprised of cultural, religious, socioeconomic, and regional references. Consequently, one must translate not with a judgmental view, but with the perception that the task of the translator is to produce a target text that allows the force and play of the original to function within newer linguistic contexts. Translation provides a site where the reconciliation of languages can take place, where a dialogue of opposites, an enantiodromia, can be brought about. This trope for translation also describes the message of the saints: the marriage of opposites—source text and target text unite in order to form a third possibility that perpetually exists between the source text and all of its potential translations (the endless array of target texts). As a third text, these translations of the songs of the saints of The Adi Granth find a metonymic linkage with the entire agenda of the Sikh holy book, in that both seek to elaborate an ideal—the former literary and the latter spiritual. The meeting ground of the two is also a union—the confluence of "this" (the source text) and "that" (the target text)—a metaphor (Greek for translation) well-embedded in the songs of these saints.[27]

Some may deem these songs as hardly poetic. It is, however, important to note that we cannot impose a preconceived aesthetic upon these songs. If we do not find them "poetic," then we must really ask what it is that we mean by the "poetic" and what elements determine its existence within any body of work. Further, we must note that aside from their melic orientation as songs to be sung as hymns, the concern of these saints is not to engage in "poeticity" as such. Rather, their agenda is broader than mere aesthetic harmony—for they are propounding an urgent and serious doctrine—the salvation of the human soul. Thus to demand a conjectured aesthetic from these songs is to miss the point: these songs are doctrinal sermons, they are not pretty songs, and their message is carried with the force and solemnity of music, not for purposes of pleasure, but in order to teach the unyielding heart: "Do not touch the safflower, / O my dearest friend, / for soon it shall fade away" (Sheikh Farid, *Raga Suhi-Lalit*, p. 209). For these saints, aesthetic pleasures are fleeting; only pleasure in the Divine lasts an eternity.

Notes

1. The Adi Granth contains 5,867 songs, proverbs, and paeans authored by six gurus, fifteen saints, and twenty-one poets and bards employed by the gurus. *The Rig Veda* contains 1,023 hymns, composed by diverse singer-poets.

2. The sant (mendicant) tradition of northern India was never homogenous and tended to attract people from the lower castes. It was, however, united in its fervent opposition to Brahminism and to organized religion, both of which constructed their identity by exclusion of the other. See W. M. McLeod, *Sikhism* (New York: Penguin, 1998); and Sunita Puri, *Advent of Sikhism: A Socio-Political Perspective* (New Delhi, India: Munshiram Manoharlal Publishers Pvt., 1993).

3. The sants especially criticized the traditional view that if one is to find God, one must abandon the world, retreat into a forest, become a hermit (sanyasi), and there meditate. The sants saw such discipline as useless and gave it the analogy of the musk deer that roams all over but does not know that the musk is inside its own navel. Austerities served no purpose, for the sants, other than to aggrandize the practitioner. See Kartar S. Duggal, *Philosophy and Faith of Sikhism* (Honesdale, PA: Himalayan Institute Press, 1988).

4. By nam Sikh theology means "universal consciousness." By meditating upon the nam, the individual contemplates the ground of all consciousness and thereby reaches the ideal state of personal awareness. This definition is similar to the Buddhist doctrine of nam; cf. nam-rupa that means the "self." See McLeod, *Historical Dictionary of Sikhism*. Historical Dictionary of Religions, Philosophies, and Movements, no. 5 (Lanham, MD: Scarecrow Press, 1995); and W. Owen and Piara Singh Sambhi, *A Popular Dictionary of Sikhism* (Lincolnwood, IL: NTC Publishing Group, 1997).

5. Cf. the Buddhist notion of the *boddhisatva*, that is, the perfected one who remains in the world as a helper. See Robert C. Lester, *Buddhism: The Path of Nirvana* (Prospect Heights, IL: Waveland Press, 1998).

6. By vernacular I mean santbhasha (also called sadhukhari or santboli), that is, "the language of holy men" that was the lingua franca of fakirs and mendicants in northern India. Its basis was the dialect of Hindi spoken around Delhi (khariboli), with dialectical influences from Avadhi, Rajasthani, Panjabi, Braj, Kosali, Bhojpuri, and even elements of Bengali.

7. See Harjot Oberoi, *The Construction of Religious Boundaries: Culture, Identity and Diversity in the Sikh Tradition* (Clarendon; New York: Oxford University Press, 1997); and McLeod, *Guru Nanak and the Sikh Religion* (Clarendon; New York: Oxford University Press, 1996) for a discussion on Nathism. See also J. S. Hawley and M. Juergensmeyer, *Songs of the Saints of India* (Clarendon; New York: Oxford University Press, 1988). Tantricism focuses on the female creative energy of the god Shiva, namely Shakti, which is deemed the true animator. The union of Shiva and Shakti serves as an important metaphor for the sants in their own description of the merging of the soul with God. See Paul Edwards Muller-Ortego, *The Triadic Heart of Siva: Tantricism of Abhinavagupta in the Non-Dual Shaivism of Kashmir*. SUNY Series in the Shaiva Traditions of Kashmir (Albany: State University of New York Press, 1989). See also Nikky-Guninder Kaur Singh, *The Feminine Principle in the Sikh Vision of the Transcendent*. Cambridge Studies in Religious Traditions, no. 3 (Cambridge: Cambridge University Press, 1993).

8. Yoga (yoke) is spiritual and physical training, comprising eight stages: self-control; attentiveness; postures; breath, sense, and mind control; contemplation; and intense meditation. Hatha-yoga (yoga of force), which is also called kundalini-yoga (yoga of the spiral), is intensely physical and stresses breath control and certain postures of the body. See Ian Whichler, *The Integrity of the Yoga Darsana: A Reconsideration of Classical Yoga*. SUNY Series in Religious Studies (Albany: State University of New York Press, 1998).

9. The chief proponent of this view is McLeod. See his *Evolution of the Sikh Community* (Oxford: Clarendon Press, 1975); and *The Sikhs: History, Religion, and Society*. Lectures on the History of Religions, New Series, no. 14 (New York: Columbia University Press, 1989).

10. See Khushwant Singh, *A History of the Sikhs*, vol. 1 (Delhi, India: Oxford University Press, 1977). McLeod (1975), pp. 1–19 disagrees with this classification and calls it an oversimplification, although unconvincingly.

11. The exigencies of caste maintained that food meant for the higher castes (Brahmins and warriors) would become impure and defile the eater if handled by a member of a lower caste; even if a shadow of a low-caste person fell on the food or on the cooking area, impurity was incurred. The elimination of such caste rules and practices was the impetus for the *langar*.

12. Prince Khusrau was the son of Jahangir and the grandson of Emperor Akbar. Akbar wanted his grandson to succeed to the throne, superseding his own son Jahangir. After Akbar's death, however, Jahangir took the throne, and Khusrau in a revolt claimed the Panjab and the area that is now Afghanistan as his territory. This led to much intrigue and

strife, until Khusrau was forced to flee Delhi. As he rested in the Panjab, he met guru Arjan Dev at Taran-Taran and asked for the Guru's aid. Arjan showed him great deference and gave him a sum of money. The prince was heading for Kabul; however, before he could clear the Panjab he was captured by imperial forces and imprisoned in Delhi. He was treated kindly by his father. Later, he was killed by his brother who became the next emperor, Shah Jahan (the builder of the Taj Mahal). For his part in the Khusrau intrigue, Guru Arjan Dev was imprisoned and tortured to death. Jahangir mentions this episode in his autobiography. See Alexander Rogers, trans., Henry Beveridge, ed., *The Tuzuk-i-Jahangiri or Memoirs of Jahangir* (1909–14; rpt. New Delhi, India: Munshiram Manoharlal Publishers, 1978), pp. 72–73.

13. Tradition has it that Guru Arjan Dev commanded his son Har Gobind, from his prison cell at Lahore Fort, to take up the sword in self-defense. Accordingly, when he became the sixth guru, Har Gobind (1594–1644), organized a strong contingent of bodyguards, established a fort at Lohgarh, and sat in the Golden Temple like a king. He also wore two swords, signifying piri and miri, the spiritual and the regnal. See Khushwant Singh, *A History of the Sikhs*, vol. 1 (Delhi, India: Oxford University Press, 1977).

14. Guru Tegh Bahadur was beheaded at Delhi by the emperor Aurangzeb because the guru defended the rights of Kashmiri Hindus to retain their religion and not to convert to Islam, as the emperor demanded. See Harbans Singh, *Guru Tegh Bahadur* (New Delhi, India: Manohar Publishers & Distributors, 1994).

15. Two of Guru Gobind's sons were captured by the Mughals and bricked up alive at Sirhind; the two others died in battle at Chamkaur. After a series of disastrous clashes with the Mughal authorities, Gobind Singh left the Panjab disguised as a Muslim fakir. After the death of Emperor Aurangzeb, Gobind Singh became a friend of the next emperor, Bahadur Shah.

16. Gobind Singh took up residence at Nander by the banks of the Godavari River in Haiderabad in 1707. Here he often held disputes with various holy men. During one of these disputes, he made disrespectful remarks about Islam; one of his Afghan retainers, Gul Khan, was incensed and stabbed the guru two or three times with his dagger. Though severely wounded the guru did not die. The emperor Bahadur Shah sent Gobind Singh two bows as presents to commemorate his recovery. As the guru pulled back the bowstring of one of the bows, his wounds burst open, and he began to bleed heavily. This time, the bleeding could not be stopped. After suffering most of the night, Gobind died in the early hours of the morning, in 1708. A temple (Huzur Sahib) now marks the spot of his death at Nander; it was built by Maharaja Ranjit Singh in 1832.

17. Harold Bloom, *Kabbalah and Criticism* (New York: Seabury Press, 1975), p. 106.

18. Roland Barthes, "From Work to Text," in *Textual Strategies: Perspectives in Post-Structuralist Criticism*, ed. J. V. Harari (Ithaca: Cornell University Press, 1979), p. 75.

19. See Gurinder Singh Mann, *The Goindval Pothis: The Earliest Extant Source of the Sikh Canon*. Harvard Oriental Series, vol. 51 (Cambridge: Harvard University Press, 1997; and McLeod, *Textual Sources for the Study of Sikhism*. Textual Sources for the Study of Religion (Chicago: University of Chicago Press, 1990).

20. Guru Arjan Dev's father, Guru Ram Dass, passed over his two older sons and conferred guruship upon Arjan, his youngest son. Consequently, Arjan had to continually face opposition from his brothers. His eldest brother, Prithi Chand along with his son Manohar Dass Meharban, began to write spurious verses under the pseudonym "Nanak." (Each guru took the name "Nanak" upon assuming the spiritual seat.) These unauthorized verses caused great confusion, and there was a demand by the faithful to assemble an authentic collection of the hymns of the previous gurus and saints. Thus, Guru Arjan Dev's *Granth* served both a spiritual (in that it provided a canonized Scripture for the community) as well as a political (in that it authenticated and reified his guruship) need. See Kartar S. Duggal, *Sikh Gurus. Their Lives and Teachings* (New Delhi, India: UBS Publishers Distributors, 1993); and Hari Ram Gupta, *History of the Sikhs*, vol. 1, *The Sikh Gurus, 1469–1708* (New Delhi, India: Munshiram Manoharlal Publishers Pvt., 1984).

21. Guru Gobind Singh's compositions are contained in the *Dasam Granth* (Book of the Tenth [Master]). Gobind Singh did not consider his writings important, calling them mere wordplay; therefore, he did not incorporate his work into the body of The Adi Granth. See Dalip Singh, *Guru Gobind Singh and Khalsa Discipline* (Amritsar, India: Singh Brothers, 1992); and Gopal Singh, *Thus Spake the Tenth Master* (Patiala, India: Punjabi University, 1978).

22. For Vedic meters see David Frawley, *Wisdom of the Ancient Seers: Mantras of the Rig Veda* (Salt Lake City, UT: Morson Publishing, 1993); and Barend A. Van Nooten and Gary B. Holland, *Rig Veda: A Metrically Restored Text with an Introduction and Notes*. Harvard Oriental Series, vol. 5 (Cambridge: Harvard University Press, 1994).

23. See Winand Callewaert and Rupert Snell, eds., *According to Tradition. Hagiographical Writing in India* (Wiesbaden, Germany: Harrassowitz, 1994).

24. Fragment 16 of Empedocles. My translation is based upon H. Diels, *Die Fragmente der Vorsokrater*, 3 vols., 6th ed.(Berlin: Weidmannsche Verlagsbuchhandlung, 1951).

25. Franz Pfeiffer, *The Works of Meister Eckhardt* (Kila, MT: Kessinger Publishing, 1997), p. 8.

26. John Ruysbroeck, *The Adornment of the Spiritual Marriage*, trans. C. A. Wynschenk (New York: Dutton, 1916), 3:6.

27. For a further discussion on the target text see Nirmal Dass, *Rebuilding Babel: The Translations of W.H. Auden*, Approaches to Translation Studies, 10 (Amsterdam; Atlanta, GA: Editions Rodopi, 1992).

BIBLIOGRAPHY

Translations and Editions of The Adi Granth

Winand Callewaert. *Shri Guru Granth Sahib*. 2 vols. Delhi, India: Motilal Banarsidass, 1996.

M. A. Macauliffe. *The Sikh Religion*. 6 vols. 1909. Reprint, New Delhi, India: S. Chand & Company, 1983.

Gopal Singh. Trans. *Sri Guru Granth Sahib*. New Delhi, India: Gurdas Kapur & Sons, 1962.

Manmohan Singh. Trans. *Sri Guru Granth Sahib*. Amritsar, India: Shromani Gurdwara Parbandhak Committee, 1962–69.

Nikky-Guninder Kaur Singh. *The Name of My Beloved: Verses of the Sikh Gurus*. San Francisco: Harper, 1995.

Gurbachan Singh Talib. Trans. *Sri Guru Granth Sahib*. 4 vols. Patiala, India: Punjabi University, 1985.

E. Trumpp. Trans. *The Adi Granth*. 1877. Reprint, New Delhi, India: Munshiram Manhorlal Publishers Pvt., 1970.

General Bibliography

Roland Barthes. "From Work to Text." In *Textual Strategies: Perspectives in Post-Structuralist Criticism*, edited by J. V. Harari. Ithaca: Cornell University Press, 1979.

Harold Bloom. *Kabbalah and Criticism*. New York: Seabury Press, 1975.

Kerry Brown. Ed. *Sikh Art and Literature*. London: Routledge, 1999.

Winand Callewaert and Mukund Lath. *The Hindi Songs of Namdev*. Delhi, India: Motilal Banarsidass, 1989.

——— and B. Op de Beeck. *Nirgun-Bhakti Sagar. Devotional Hindi Literature*. Heidelberg, Germany: *Süd-Asien Institut*, 1991.

——— and P. Friedlander. *The Life and Work of Raidas*. Delhi, India: Manohar Book Publications, 1992.

——— and Rupert Snell. Eds. *According to Tradition. Hagiographical Writing in India*. Wiesbaden, Germany: Harrassowitz, 1994.

Nirmal Dass. *Songs of Kabir from the Adi Granth*. Albany: State University of New York Press, 1991. Delhi, India: Sri Satguru Publications, 1992.

———. *Rebuilding Babel: The Translations of W.H. Auden*. Approaches to Translation Studies, 10. Amsterdam; Atlanta, GA: Editions Rodopi, 1992.

H. Diels. *Die Fragmente der Vorsokrater*. 3 vols. 6th ed. Berlin: Weidmannsche Verlagsbuchhandlung, 1951.

Ramesh Chander Dogra and Gobind Singh Mansukhani. *Encyclopedia of Sikh Religion and Culture*. New Delhi, India: Vikas Publishing House, 1995.

W. C. Chittick. *The Sufi Path of Knowledge*. Albany: State University of New York Press, 1989.

Alain Daniélou. *Ragas of Northern Indian Music*. New Delhi, India: Munshiram Manoharlal, 1991.

Kartar S. Duggal. *Sikh Gurus. Their Lives and Teachings*. New Delhi, India: UBS Publishers Distributors, 1993.

———. *Philosophy and Faith of Sikhism*. Honesdale, PA: Himalayan Institute Press, 1988.

James Fadiman and Robert Frager. Eds. *Essential Sufism*. Edison, NJ: Castle Books, 1998.

David Frawley. *Wisdom of the Ancient Seers: Mantras of the Rig Veda*. Salt Lake City, UT: Morson Publishing, 1993.

J. S. Grewal. *The Sikhs of the Punjab*. New Cambridge History of India 2:3. Cambridge: Cambridge University Press, 1998.

Hari Ram Gupta. *History of the Sikhs*. Vol. 1. *The Sikh Gurus*. New Delhi, India: Munshiram Manoharlal Publishers Pvt., 1984.

J. S. Hawley and M. Juergensmeyer. *Songs of the Saints of India*. Clarendon; New York: Oxford University Press, 1988.

Robert C. Lester. *The Path of Nirvana*. Prospects Heights, IL: Waveland Press, 1998.

David N. Lorenzen. *Bhakti Religion in North India: Community, Identity and Political Action*. SUNY Series in Religious Studies. Albany: State University of New York Press, 1995.

Gurinder Singh Mann. *The Goindval Pothis: The Earliest Extant Source of the Sikh Canon*. Harvard Oriental Series, vol. 51. Cambridge: Harvard University Press, 1997.

W. M. McLeod. *Sikhism*. New York: Penguin, 1998.

———. *Guru Nanak and the Sikh Religion*. Clarendon; New York: Oxford University Press, 1996.

———. *Historical Dictionary of Sikhism*. Historical Dictionary of Religions, Philosophies, and Movements, No. 5. Lanham, MD: Scarecrow Press, 1995.

———. *Textual Sources for the Study of Sikhism*. Textual Sources for the Study of Religion. Chicago: University of Chicago Press, 1990.

———. *The Sikhs: History, Religion, and Society*. Lectures on the History of Religions, New Series, no. 14. New York: Columbia University Press, 1989.

———. *Evolution of the Sikh Community*. Clarendon: Oxford University Press, 1977.

Barend A. Van Nooten and Gary B. Holland. *Rig Veda: A Metrically Restored Text with an Introduction and Notes*. Harvard Oriental Series, vol. 5. Cambridge: Harvard University Press, 1994.

Paul Edwards Muller-Ortega. *The Triadic Heart of Siva: Tantricism of Abhinavagupta in the Non-Dual Shaivism of Kashmir*. SUNY Series in the Shaiva Traditions of Kashmir. Albany: State University of New York Press, 1989.

Harjot Oberoi. *The Construction of Religious Boundaries: Culture, Identity and Diversity in the Sikh Tradition*. Clarendon; New York: Oxford University Press, 1997.

W. Owen and Piara Singh Sambi. *A Popular Dictionary of Sikhism*. Lincolnwood, IL: NTC Publishing Group, 1997.

Franz Pfeiffer. *The Works of Meister Eckhardt*. Kila, MT: Kessinger Publishing, 1997.

Sunita Puri. *Advent of Sikhism: A Socio-Political Perspective*. New Delhi, India: Munshiram Manoharlal Publishers Pvt., 1993.

Alexander Rogers. Trans. and Henry Beveridge. Ed. *The Tuzuk-i-Jahangiri or Memoirs of Jahangir*. 1909–14. Reprint, New Delhi, India: Munshiram Manoharlal Publishers, 1978.

John Ruysbroeck. *The Adornment of the Spiritual Marriage*, translated by C. A. Wynschenk. New York: Dutton, 1916.

Karine Schomer and W. H. McLeod. Eds. *The Sant Traditions of India*. Berkeley: Berkeley Graduate Theological Union Religious Studies Series, 1983.

Dalip Singh. *Guru Gobind Singh and Khalsa Discipline*. Amritsar, India: Singh Brothers, 1992.

Gopal Singh. *Thus Spake the Tenth Master*. Patiala, India: Punjabi University, 1978.

Harbans Singh. *Guru Tegh Bahadur*. New Delhi, India: Manohar Publishers & Distributors, 1994.

Khushwant Singh. *A History of the Sikhs*. 2 vols. Delhi, India: Oxford University Press, 1977.

Nikky-Guninder Kaur Singh. *The Feminine Principle in the Sikh Vision of the Transcendent*. Cambridge Studies in Religious Traditions, no. 3. Cambridge: Cambridge University Press, 1993.

Ian Whichler. *The Integrity of the Yoga Darsana: A Reconsideration of Classical Yoga*. SUNY Series in Religious Studies. Albany: State University of New York Press, 1998.

SONGS OF THE SAINTS FROM THE ADI GRANTH

NAMDEVA

There is little room for surety when we search for factual details about Namdeva's life. What we do know can be gleaned from his sixty songs in The Adi Granth; the rest is mostly legend. These facts can be summed up briefly: he was a calico- or cotton-printer by caste, and as such was a shudra, the lowest in the Hindu caste system. Because of his caste, he was often thrown out from temples, which were forbidden to members of the lower castes. He was once forced to convert to Islam by a Muslim ruler, perhaps Muhammad bin Tughlaq (1325–51), whom he successfully overcame with the sincerity of his own faith. This is the bare bones life of Namdeva.

Legend claims that he traveled the length and breadth of India, visiting various shrines in order to acquire spiritual knowledge. One day he came to Pandharpur where stood a temple to the god Bithal (one of Krishna's incarnations). This shrine commemorated Krishna's own thirst for spiritual knowledge in that he visited this spot in order to meet the holy sage Pandarika. However, the sage was too busy with his meditations to talk to Krishna and instead threw him a brick upon which to stand. Lost in meditation, Pandarika completely forgot about Krishna, who did not step down from the brick. Many years passed. Pandarika still meditated, and Krishna still stood waiting for an audience. Before long, people began to gather to see the unmoving pair, and they began to call Krishna Bithal (he who stands upon a brick). A cult of Bithal eventually developed and the city of Pandharpur was established.

Like Krishna, Namdeva also remained at Pandharpur, and eventually died in the city; his ashes were also interred there. A stone now marks the sight.

Namdeva's dates are usually given as 1270–1350. His birth place is said to be the village of Narsi, in the district of Satara, southeast of Bombay city (present-day Mumbai), in Maharashtra Province.

But there also exists a shrine to Namdeva in the village of Ghuman, in the Panjab, in the district of Gurdaspur. Tradition claims that this is the same Namdeva as the one from Bombay, and during his travels he came to the Panjab, stayed on, and died there. The shrine marks the place where he was cremated. Thus, the Panjab and Maharashtra both claim the saint.

The language of the songs is mostly santbhasha, with a large mixture of Old Marathi and southern Apabhramsa. Traces of Sindhi and Gujrati are also discernible. Two of the songs are in Persian that was the lingua franca of northern India during the Muslim rule.

THE SONGS OF NAMDEVA

Raga Gauri-Cheti

Stones floated because of You, O Deva.
So why can't a man float across
to the other side of death by saying, "Ram"? (Rest)

It was You who saved that prostitute,
that misshapen, hunched girl,
that great sinner Ajamala,
that hunter who shot the fatal arrow.
How I cherish all those who utter, "Ram."

Vidura, the slave-girl's son,
Sudama, Ugarsaina—all became kings.
All those without piety, devotion,
high lineage, or goodness—
Namdeva's Swami floated them all across.

Raga Asa

1.

He is the One in many,
countless are His shapes and forms.
He pervades all that exists:
wherever I look, He is there.
But very few perceive this reality,
for Maya ever enchants us
with her mutable reflections
of color and alluring beauty.

Everything is Gobind,
Gobind is everything.
Nothing that exists
is without Gobind:
the one thread strings
innumerable beads—
Prabhu Himself is the thread,
the threader, the threaded. (Rest)

River and waves,
foam and bubbles
have all their being
within water itself.
This play of things
is the sport of Parbhama.
The One cannot be thought
different from the other.

Hope is a lie
and desire a mere dream—
yet both are construed
as actual reality.
But when my guru
gave me his holy wisdom,
I awoke from my dream
and my heart yielded.

Namdeva says,
Behold Hari's creation;
ponder upon it
with all your heart,
And you will see
that in every pore,
in every living thing,
there is only the one Murari.

2.

I brought a pitcher,
filled it with water,
so I could bathe the idol.
But four million,
two hundred thousand beings
call water their home.
How can I bathe Bithal,
who existed before all others?

Wherever I turn,
I find Bithal hidden away,
joyful in his sport,
filled with bliss. (Rest)

I brought some flowers
and strung them into a garland
so I could adorn the idol.
But the fragrance of these flowers
was first smelled
and enjoyed by the bee.
How can I adorn Bithal,
who existed before all others?

I brought some milk
and made a sweet pudding from it,
so I could place it as an offering
before the idol.
But the milk was first
suckled by the calf.
How can I offer it to Bithal,

who existed before all others?
Bithal is here below,
Bithal is up above,
without Bithal
the world cannot be.
This is Namdeva's plea:
in every nook and cranny,
in each speck of creation,
there is You.

3.

I have made my heart a yardstick
and my tongue is a pair of scissors:
measure by measure, I cut away
the noose of Yama.

What use is caste to me?
What use a high lineage?
I only know how to worship
The name of Ram. (Rest)

I have dyed what needed dying
and sewn what needed sewing.
Now I cannot live one moment
without the name of Ram.

My worship is singing
the praises of Hari.
At each watch of the day and night
I long for my Master.

With a golden needle
and a silver thread,
Namdeva's soul
is sewn to Hari.

4.

The snake sheds its skin,
but not its poison,

just as a crane stands in water
looking deep within.

Why meditate, why worship
when my heart is not pure? (Rest)

The man who only knows
how to ravage like a lion
is always called
the greatest of thugs.

But Namdeva's Swami
has settled the quarrel:
come and drink Ram's ambrosia,
O all you who are stone-hearted.

5.

Those who recognize Parbrahma's reality
do not need false promises and hopes.
The saintly souls who ponder upon Ram
are freed from all fears and worries.

Brothers, how can my heart swim across
when the waters of this world-ocean are poisoned?
When my heart beheld the false grandeur of Maya
it lost itself entirely. (Rest)

I was born in the house of a calico-printer,
but still I gained revelation from my guru,
and now by the grace of saints,
I, Namdeva, have found Hari.

Raga Gujri

1.

Though I rule a great kingdom
where is my greatness?
And if I go about begging food
how am I fallen?

Praise Hari, O my soul,
until you are saved.
Then never again
will you come and go. (Rest)

It was You who created all things,
and it was You who cast us into illusion.
Those whom You allow
guess this great riddle.

Upon finding the True Guru,
heart-gripping fear vanishes.
So whom should I really worship?
I can see no other.

People will worship and love one stone,
while another they will trample underfoot.
If stone is God, then all stones are God.
But, O Namdeva, say, I serve only the true Hari.

2.

No stain sullies Him,
for He is beyond stains.
He is unseen
like fragrance in a flower,
O my sister.
No one sees

His comings and goings.
Who can know Him, O my sister?

Who can describe Him?
Who can find Him out?
He who is my beautiful Ram,
O my sister. (Rest)

Though you see
a bird against the sky,
yet you cannot see
the path it follows.
Though you see
a fish swimming in water,
yet you cannot see
the course it traces.

Like a hart
pricked and driven by thirst
chases after a mirage of water
on a horizon ever-receding.
Such is Namdeva's Swami,
the Lord Bithal,
whose ways cannot be known,
who burns away all trace.

Raga Sorath

1.

When I see His ways, I sing.
Thus I find peace, O brothers.

O brothers, lose yourself in the Word;
the true guru shall lead you to Deva. (Rest)

Where light shimmers,
there resounds the unsounded Word.

Light blends with light:
this I perceived by the guru's grace.

There were rubies bright as lightning
in my own lotus-room.

He is near, not far.
He fills my very breath.

Where shines the eternal Sun,
there a lamp also dimly burns.

I finally understood by the guru's grace.
Now the slave Namdeva is blended with the Eternal.

2.

A neighboring woman asks Namdeva,
"Who built this cottage for you?
I will pay this carpenter twice the labor
if you send him to me."

"O my sister,
I cannot send you this Carpenter,

for behold, He is everywhere.
My Carpenter is the brace of my soul." (Rest)

"This Carpenter wants love as His wage,
if you want Him to build you a cottage.
Break free from this world, from your kinsmen,
And the Carpenter Himself will come to you.

"Such a Carpenter cannot be described,
He is everywhere, in everything.
Just as a mute when he drinks the sweetest nectar
cannot describe what he is tasting.

"O my sister,
hear the virtues of this Carpenter:
He bound the oceans and fixed Dhruva
and gave Lanka to Vibhishana to rule."

3.

The drum with no drumhead beats;
clouds thunder without the monsoon;
rain falls without clouds.
Can anyone guess this riddle?

I have met Ram the beautiful,
and I too have become beautiful. (Rest)

The philosopher's stone turns lead into gold;
costly rubies I string with my words and thoughts.
I discovered real love; doubts, fears have left me.
I found comfort in what my guru taught me.

A pitcher will fill when plunged in water,
so Ram is the One in all.
The guru's heart and the disciple's heart are one.
Thus has the slave Namdeva perceived Truth.

Raga Dhanashri

1.

A splendid palace built upon deep foundations;
yet who lived longer than Markanda
who himself whiled away his life
with mere wattle and mud over his head.

The Creator Ram is my Beloved.
O my brothers,
why are you so filled with pride?
This false body will one day crumble away. (Rest)

"Mine, mine," said the Kauravas—
Duryodhana and all his brothers;
their army covered forty-eight miles.
And still vultures ate their bodies.

Lanka was made all of gold,
and who was stronger than Ravana?
Where now are all the elephants tied at his door?
In a trice all that was his became someone else's.

When they deceived Durvasa
the Yadavas got the fruit of their actions.
Have mercy on Your slave,
for Namdeva ever sings Hari's praise.

2.

I overcame the ten ascetics
and erased the five completely.
The seventy-two I filled with ambrosia,
thrashing out the poison.

I shall not come back here again,
for my heart sings

sweet, holy words
with which I teach my soul. (Rest)

I have hacked away
at my hardness with an ax.
Pleading, I fall at His feet.
I honor and revere saints.

I shall only be freed from this world
when I stop embracing Maya.
Birth, the womb—these are Maya.
Forsaking her, I come to perceive Him.

The man who practices such devotion
shall be freed from all fear.
Namdeva says, Why wander and roam about?
Find Hari by methods such as these.

3.

As water is dear in Marwar,
and the creeper dear to a camel;
as a hunter's horn is dear
to a stag at night—
so is the beautiful Ram dear to my heart.

Beautiful is Your name, beautiful Your face,
beautiful Your hue, O my precious Ram. (Rest)

As Indra is dear to the earth,
and the scent of the lotus
dear to the bumblebee;
as a mango-tree is dear to the cuckoo—
so is the beautiful Ram dear to my heart.

As the sun is dear to a *chakava*-bird
and Lake Mansarowar
dear to a swan;
as a husband is dear to a young wife—
so is the beautiful Ram dear to my heart.

As milk is dear to a young child,
and the fall of rain
dear to a *chatrik*'s beak;
as water is dear to a fish—
so is the beautiful Ram dear to my heart.

Holy men, ascetics, hermits—
all yearn for Him—
but few see Him;
as Your name is dear to all the world—
so is Bithal dear to Namdeva's heart.

4.

In the first of beginnings
was created the white lotus;
its petals were the beings of all creation.
Behold, Maya emanates from Hari,
and she, Hari's dancing girl,
is raptly dancing.

First God appeared,
and from His being came Maya.
From That into this.
This is Hari's garden,
where water dances
in brimming well-pots. (Rest)

Maids and men dance;
they are not different
from the Dancer.
Do not doubt.
Do not fear.
Keshava's Word animates each being.

The well-pot rises
and plunges into the world.
Lost and wandering I came to Your door.
"Who are you, O man?"
I, Lord, am
Namdeva,

O Lord.
Save me from this world, and from Yama.

5.

Making sin holy
is Your true essence, O Madho.
Happy are the saints and sages
who meditate upon my Lord Hari.

The dust from Gobind's feet
marks my forehead—
that dust which is unattainable
by mighty warriors, heroes or sages. (Rest)

O Madho, merciful to the poor,
destroyer of pride—
it is the shelter of Your feet
that Namdeva seeks, offering himself to You.

Raga Todi

1.

Some say He is near,
others say He is far:
a fish from a river
climbs up a palm-tree.

What's the point
of this useless quarrel?
Those who find Hari
hide Him away. (Rest)

A pundit may wax profound
about the Vedas.
But the fool Namdeva
only knows a little about Hari.

2.

Whose sin remains in tact
the moment he utters Ram's name?
Sinners become holy
the moment they cry out "Ram." (Rest)

By embracing Ram
the slave Namdeva believed.
Why now should I fast every month
and go on pilgrimages?

Namdeva says,
Good are my deeds, pure my heart.
By following the guru's path,
by uttering "Ram," who has not gone to heaven?

3.

This is the play of three things. (Rest)

A pot belongs in a potter's house,
elephants belong in a king's palace;
horoscopes belong in a Brahmin's house—
horoscopes, pots, elephants, ho!

Spices belong in a merchant's house,
horns belong on a bull's head;
a *lingam* belongs in Shiva's house—
lingam, horns, spices, ho!

Oil belongs in an oiler's house,
vines belong in a jungle;
a banana-tree belongs in a gardener's house—
bananas, vines, oil, ho!

Gobind belongs in a saint's house,
Shyama belongs in Gokul;
Ram belongs inside Namdeva—
Ram, Shyama, Gobind, ho!

Raga Tilang

1.

For me, a blind man,
Your name is my support, O King.
I am poor, I am wretched.
Your name is my support. (Rest)

You are merciful,
You are forgiving.
O Allah, You are kind.
You are present everywhere.
You are always before me.

You are a river, a giver;
Your treasure is endless.
You give. You take away.
You are ever unchanging.
There is none but You.

You are all-wise.
You are all-seeing.
I am poor. What can I do?
O Namdeva's Lord,
You are the forgiving Hari.

2.

Hail, Friend, hail Friend.
Is all well? I honor You, I honor You.
Good are Your works,
exalted Your name. (Rest)

Where have You come from?
Where have You been? Where are You going?
This is Dwarka city,
where You must speak the truth.

Handsome is Your turban,
and sweet Your words.
But why does a Mongol
come here to Dwarka city?

Among the thousands here,
there is only one Khan.
I think I have spied out
the King with the dusky hue.

The lord of horses,
the lord of elephants,
the lord of men—these You rule.
Namdeva's Master is Lord and Savior.

Raga Bilawal

The guru made my life fruitful;
I forgot suffering and gained peace.

The guru put wisdom's kohl in my eyes:
without Ram's name life and heart are empty. (Rest)

Namdeva perceived Him through meditation,
and now my soul has blended with His soul.

Raga Gaund

1.

Performing the horse sacrifice,
giving your weight in alms,
bathing at Prayag—

none of these is better, O Namdeva,
than singing the praises of Hari.
O my foolish heart,
praise your wondrous Ram. (Rest)

Offering grain at Gaya,
dwelling by the Asi in Benares,
reading all the four Vedas—

none of these is better, O Namdeva,
than singing the praises of Hari.
O my foolish heart,
praise your wondrous Ram.

Observing all the rituals,
restraining passion with the guru's wisdom,
fulfilling the six duties—

none of these is better, O Namdeva,
than singing the praises of Hari.
O my foolish heart,
praise your wondrous Ram.

Reading Shiva's dialogues—
O my heart, leave, leave all this folly,
and praise, praise Gobind.

Worship Him, O Namdeva,
and you shall swim across
this world's ocean.

2.

Like a stag follows a hunter's horn,
losing its life, yet still intently listening.

Thus ever I look upon Ram;
my thoughts do not leave Ram
and wander to other things. (Rest)

Like a crane looks at a fish,
like a goldsmith looks at gold he shapes.

Like a man lusts after a woman,
like a gambler looks at dice.

Wherever I look, Ram is there.
Namdeva ever worships at Hari's feet.

3.

Carry me over, O Ram, carry me over.
I am an ignorant man who cannot swim.
O father Bithal, give me Your arm. (Rest)

Man becomes god in an instant,
when the guru gives him wisdom.
Born of man, yet I conquer heaven,
having drunk a wondrous tonic.

Where You placed Narada and Dhruva,
there ever place me.
Clinging to Your Name, many were carried over:
such is Namdeva's personal wisdom.

4.

Such is my great longing:
as a cow without her calf pines.

Without water, a fish writhes—
such is poor Namdeva without Ram's name. (Rest)

Like a young calf turned loose
runs to suck teats filled with rich milk—

thus Namdeva has found Narayana,
when the guru made visible the Unseen.

Like a lust-driven man looking at a woman—
such is Namdeva's love for Murari.

Like specks dancing in pure sunlight—
so is poor Namdeva without Ram's name.

5.

By saying Hari, Hari,
all doubts vanish.
Repeating Hari's name
is the highest religion.
By saying Hari, Hari
caste and lineage vanish.
Hari is the blind man's staff.

I praise Hari, I bow before Him.
By saying Hari, Hari
Yama's pain vanishes. (Rest)

Hari took the life of Harnakhasa
and gave Ajamala
a place in heaven.
The prostitute gained salvation
by teaching her parrot.
This is the Hari
most dear to my eyes.

By saying Hari, Hari, Putana was saved—
she who was a child-slayer
and filled with evil deceit.
By remembering Him,
Draupada's daughter was saved.
Gautama's wife, though turned to stone,
also swam across.

He who destroyed Kesi and Kamsa
and gave breath back to Kaliya.
To that very Hari
Namdeva makes his supplications;
praising Him banishes
all fear and hardship.

6.

Devotees of Bhairava
shall become demons;
devotees of Sitala
shall ride donkeys,
merely raising dust.

As for me, I shall take Ram the beautiful,
giving all other gods in exchange. (Rest)

Those who worship
by saying, "Shiva, Shiva"
will mount oxen
and go about beating
great big kettledrums.

Those who worship
the Great Mother
will all be changed
from men
into mere women.

You call yourself
the primal Bhavani.
But when it was time
for salvation,
where did you go and hide?

Follow the guru's wisdom,
O my dear friend,
and grab hold of Ram's name.
Namdeva knows as well
that this is what the *Gita* says.

Raga Bilawal-Gaund

7.

Today Namdeva beheld Bithal.
How can I explain to fools? (Rest)

O pundit, your Gayatri
once grazed the field of some Lodha.
He took a staff and broke her leg;
thereafter she limped as she walked.

O pundit, I saw your Mahadeva
riding a white bull,
going to a merchant's house for a feast.
But he killed that merchant's son.

O pundit, I also saw your Ram Chandra;
he was fighting with Ravana
because he had lost
the woman of his house.

Hindus are blind
and Turks one-eyed.
Wiser than both
is the one enlightened.

Hindus worship in temples,
Muslims worship in mosques.
Namdeva worships Him
who lives in neither.

Raga Ramkali

1.

A boy takes some paper,
cuts it, and makes a kite,
making it soar high in the sky.
Though the boy is busy
talking to his friends,
his attention is ever on the string.

My heart is strung to Ram's name,
like a goldsmith ever intent with gold. (Rest)

A girl takes a pitcher
to the well outside the village
and fills it with water.
She laughs and jokes and talks
with all the other girls—
but she never forgets her own pitcher.

If all the cows of a great house
with ten high gates
are let loose to graze,
and they wander for ten miles
seeking pasture—yet each one
shall remember her calf when she returns.

Namdeva says,
Listen, O Trilochan,
a baby may lie in the cradle
and his mother may go about
doing this or that—
but her mind is intent on her child.

2.

I shall not sing and chant
the endless verses

of the *Vedas*, *Puranas* and *Shastras,*
for in the realm of perfection,
before Nirankar,
I play the soundless flute.

Forsaking all others,
I shall sing of Ram,
steeped in the asceticism
of the deathless Word,
and I shall go to the house
of the All-pervasive. (Rest)

By closing the breaths
of the right nostril
and the left nostril
at the bridge of my nose,
and by balancing the moon with the sun,
I shall find Brahma's light.

I do not go on pilgrimages,
I do not bathe in holy pools,
nor bother the creatures living there.
The guru himself showed me
the sixty-eight shrines:
I shall bathe within my own body.

I do not hunger
for praise or admiration
from friends or strangers.
Namdeva says,
My mind is steeped in Hari:
I shall blend with Silence.

3.

When there was no mother,
when there was no father.
When there was no Karma,
when there was no body.
When I did not exist,
and you did not exist,
then how, and from where, did we come?

O Ram, no one belongs to anyone:
like a tree is home to many birds. (Rest)

When there was no moon,
when there was no sun,
when water and air
were yet unparted.
When there were no *Vedas*,
when there were no *Shastras*,
from where did Karma arise?

Drawing up breath
and drawing down breath,
the necklace of sweet basil—
all these I have,
by the guru's grace.
Namdeva says, He is Primal Essence.
The true guru showed Him to me.

4.

Though you perform penance
in the Benarsi style,
standing on your head.
Though you die at a holy place
and your body be burnt with fire.
Though you rejuvenate your body
by some wondrous means.
Though you perform
the great horse sacrifice,
and make offerings of gold
in pious secrecy—
you still shall not attain Ram's name.

Leave, leave, O vain heart,
all this deception.
Don't lie to yourself.
Always, always speak Hari's name. (Rest)

Though you go to the Ganges,
and though you go

to the banks of the Godavari.
Though you go to the Kumbh festival,
and though you bathe at Kedara.
Though you offer
countless cows at Gomti,
and though you go
on endless pilgrimages.
Though you freeze yourself
in the snows of the Himalayas—
you still shall not attain Ram's name.

Though you give away
all your horses,
and though you give away
all your elephants.
Though you give away
your great canopied beds,
and though you give away
your women and your lands.
Though you offer
your own soul to the gods,
and make yourself like purified gold—
you still shall not attain Ram's name.

Do not let your heart grieve
with great sorrow,
nor blame everything
on Yama alone.
Learn to recognize
that pure state of Nirvana.
Namdeva says,
come and drink
great drafts of ambrosia
from that eternal spring—
King Jasrath's son,
my own Ram Chandra.

Raga Maligaura

1.

Beautifully, wondrously
sounds the flute of Ram.
A sonorous, divine melody
echoes softly, sweetly. (Rest)

Praised be that flock of sheep
from whose wool was made
that beautiful cloak
worn by Krishna.

Hail, hail, O mother Devaki!
In your home was born
the beautiful Ram,
the Lord of Kamla.

Blessed, blessed
be that forest Bindraban,
where the Lord Narayana
played and frolicked.

The flute plays,
the cows graze.
Namdeva's Lord
ever works bliss.

2.

O my father, Madho,
You are worthy of praise,
O Keshava, O dusky Bithal. (Rest)

Holding the discus,
You descended from heaven,

and saved the elephant's life.
In the court of Duhshasana,
You preserved Draupadi's honor,
whose clothes were being torn off.

You saved Ahlaya,
the wife of Gautama.
You have cleansed and saved
countless many.
The low-born, casteless Namdeva
comes seeking Your protection.

3.

In each and every pore
speaks Ram, only Ram.
Without Ram who can speak,
O my brother? (Rest)

From the one clay—
elephants and ants.
Many are the vessels,
O my brother.

Trees, mountains, rocks,
in all living beings that move,
even in insects and moths—
in all these is Ram compounded.

Hold the Eternal One in your thoughts.
Forsake all others, O my brother.
Namdeva says, I am freed from desire:
who is now the Master and who the slave?

Raga Maru

All salvation and all power
is found in the abode
of the Bridegroom.
Thus shall you be saved
and acquire great fame
throughout the ages.
Men shall sing your praise,
and a royal umbrella
shall shade your head.

Who, who cannot be saved
by remembering Raja Ram?
Follow the guru's way,
sit among holy men,
and you too shall be called
a pious devotee. (Rest)

The conch, discus, garland,
the sacred mark on the forehead
shall become visible.
Seeing their glory,
Yama shall take fright.
Then shall you become fearless,
Ram's strength shall thunder,
and the pain of birth and death
shall be forever stilled.

He gave this fearlessness
to Ambarika,
and exalted the reign
of Vibhishana.
The Lord gave to Sudama
all the nine treasures.
And He situated Dhruva,
unmoving forever,
where he remains to this day.

For the love of His follower,
He slew Harnakhasa,
after taking on
the shape and form
of Narsingh.
Namdeva says,
Keshava obeys His disciples:
behold, He still stands
at Bali's door.

Raga Bhairo

1.

O my brother,
I would cut my tongue
into a hundred pieces,
if it did not say,
Lord Gobind.

With Hari's name
I have stained my tongue.
How beautiful is that stain
of Hari, Hari. (Rest)

Other words are useless
on my tongue.
The name of the one Hari
is salvation.

Were I to worship
a hundred million others,
I would not come close
to adoring Hari's name.

Namdeva says,
Speak these words:
endless are your forms,
O Narayana.

2.

He who forsakes coveting
another man's wealth and wife,
in him dwells the Lord of men.

Those who do not honor Narayana,
I do not even look upon them. (Rest)

Those whose hearts
are distant from Him
are like mere animals.

Namdeva says, He who lacks a nose
cannot be called handsome
though his limbs be comely.

3.

A bowl full of milk,
a jug of water.
Namdeva was milking his white cow.

Drink some milk,
O my king Gobind.
Drink some milk,
and comfort my heart.
Otherwise my father
will be very upset.

Namdeva took a golden bowl
filled with ambrosial milk
and placed it before Him.

Love for Him fills my heart.
Seeing Namdeva,
Narayana smiled.

When He drank the milk,
the worshipper went home.
Thus Namdeva beheld Hari.

4.

I am mad,
but Ram is my husband.
With great care
I adorn myself for Him.

People can curse me,
can curse me, can curse me.
But my heart and body
cling to my beloved Ram. (Rest)

I do not quarrel or argue
with anyone at all.
For I am rapt with licking
Ram's ambrosia with my tongue.

Only I really know
the state I am in.
Come, meet me, O Gopal.
Why should we care what others say.

Some praise me,
others curse me—
but Namdeva has now met
Srirang, the Lover of Lakshmi.

5.

At times, you have so much
milk, sugar, and butter
that they are tasteless.
At other times,
you beg for a crust of bread,
from house to house.
And sometimes,
you pick through garbage,
or gather meager grain
left by others.

O my brother,
be happy where Ram has put you.
Hari's greatness
cannot easily be described. (Rest)

At times,
you let your Turkish horse
dance and frolic.

At other times,
you don't even have shoes
for your feet.
Sometimes, you sleep
on a bed with white silk sheets.
And then, you don't even have straw
for the hard ground.

Namdeva says,
His one Name alone
can carry us across.
If you meet the right guru,
he shall carry you along.

6.

With laughter and joy
I came to Your temple.
As he worshipped,
they grabbed and pushed Namdeva out.

Low is my caste,
O King of the Yadavas.
Why was I born
a calico-printer? (Rest)

I took my mat
and went back outside,
and far behind the temple
I sat down.

As Namdeva sang
the praises of Hari,
the temple itself turned
and faced His devoted slave.

7.

Like the starving love food,
like the thirsty need water,

like a fool clings to his family—
such is Namdeva's love for Narayana.

Namdeva has fallen in love with Narayana.
How easily he has forsaken the world. (Rest)

Like a lustful woman smitten by a stranger,
like the greedy forever craving money,
like a woman to a lecherous man—
such is Namdeva's love for Murari.

Only He Himself can grant true love;
all doubt flees by the guru's grace.
Such love never fades, it is infinite—
Namdeva meditates upon His true Name.

Like the love between a child and a mother—
thus is my heart filled with Hari.
Namdeva says, I have fallen in love:
Gobind dwells in my soul.

8.

A blind man leaves his own wife
and sleeps with another woman—
like a parrot
eager for the silk tree:
in the end,
it dies hanging.

A sinner's abode will be fire.
He shall burn, but not be consumed. (Rest)

He does not go where Hari is praised;
he leaves the right path and goes astray.
He forgets the Root Cause of all things,
and thus wanders in the circle of life and death:
forsaking the wellspring of ambrosia,
he drifts away and drinks poison.

Like a dancing whore
performing in her brothel,

beautifully dressed and made-up.
Rhythmically she sways,
sweetly she sings.
But around her neck is Yama's noose.

Those whose fate
is already written down—
they should all run
and seek the guru's protection.
This is what Namdeva thinks:
O saints, such is the way to salvation.

9.

Sanda and Marka
went and said:
"He doesn't want to study,
and we're tired of teaching him.
All he does
is clap and sing about Ram.
And he's corrupting
the other students as well.

"He's forever repeating Ram's name.
He has placed the Lord Hari in his heart." (Rest)

The queen, his mother,
pleaded and said:
"He has conquered
the whole world."
But her son, Prahlada,
would not listen to her at all.
He had something else
in his heart.

His enemies all gathered together
and vowed to kill him:
they threw him down a mountain,
felled a tree upon him,
tossed him into water and fire—
but Raja Ram changed the very nature

of these elements,
so they did not harm him.

In anger his father drew his sword,
and threatened to kill him:
"Tell me, who shall save you now?"
Then Hari Himself
spoke from the pillar:
"The yellow-robed One,
the Holder of the three worlds
shall save him."

He who tore apart Harnakhasa
with his claws,
and was the support
of gods and men,
say Namdeva, That Hari
I shall praise, that Ram,
who bestows fearlessness
upon us all.

10.

The Sultan asked,
"Listen, you Namdeva,
show me the works
of your Ram."

The Sultan had Namdeva bound.
"Show me your Hari Bithal." (Rest)

Give life back
to this slaughtered cow,
or I'll slit your throat
right here and now!"

"O great king,
how can this be?
No one can restore life
to something that is dead.

"There is nothing within my power
that I can now do.
That which Ram ordains
comes to pass."

The king's great anger
grew hotter,
and he ordered an elephant
be brought to trample me.

Namdeva's mother
pleaded with him:
"Forsake Ram
and praise Khuda."

"I am not your son,
nor are you my mother.
Though my body be destroyed,
yet shall I sing Hari's praise."

The giant elephant
struck with his trunk.
But Namdeva was saved
by Hari's shield.

Next, the *qazis* and *mullahs*
made obeisance to the Sultan,
saying: "This Hindu
has ruined our pride."

"O great king,
hear our plea:
take Namdeva's weight
in gold, and release him."

"Shall I take a bribe
and go to hell?
Shall I forsake my faith
for the good of the world?"

They shackled his feet,
bound his hands.

But Namdeva continued singing
the praises of Gopal.

Though the Ganges and the Jamuna
flow backwards,
yet shall Namdeva
keep repeating "Hari."

When the seventh hour struck,
the Holder
of the three worlds
still did not appear.

Then beating his wings
Garuda came flying;
riding him
was Gobind Himself.

He is the Keeper
of His followers;
mounted upon Garuda,
Gopal came.

"Say the word,
and the world shall be upturned.
Say the world,
and I shall carry it aloft.

"Say the word,
and I shall give life
to the dead cow—
so that all may believe."

Namdeva said,
"Tie her hoof,
and bring her calf;
milk her that it may drink."

When the pail
filled with milk,
they took it
and put it before the king.

The king went inside
his palace,
and the hour of affliction
came upon him.

He begged
through his *qazis* and *mullahs*:
"Forgive me, O Hindu,
I am your cow."

Namdeva said,
"Listen, O great king,
Remember
only this—

"The purpose of this miracle
was that you, O Sultan,
should walk
the path of truth and humility."

Everywhere
people spoke of Namdeva.
All the Hindus gathered
and came to Namdeva—

"If the cow had not been made
to live again,
all Namdeva's merit
would have been lost."

Namdeva's fame
shall ever remain upon the earth.
He shall cross over,
taking lovers of God with him.

Affliction and pain
befell the mockers:
now there is no difference
between Namdeva and Narayana.

11.

If you have a gracious guru,
you shall meet Murari.
If you have a gracious guru,
you shall go across.
If you have a gracious guru,
you shall go to heaven.
If you have a gracious guru,
you shall die to the world.

True, true, true, true, true
is the gracious guru.
False, false, false, false
is the service of any other. (Rest)

If you have a gracious guru,
you shall hold firm His Name.
If you have a gracious guru,
you shall not roam aimlessly.
If you have a gracious guru,
you shall be freed from desire.
If you have a gracious guru,
you shall not die of grief.

If you have a gracious guru,
you shall possess the ambrosial Word.
If you have a gracious guru,
you shall know the untold tale.
If you have a gracious guru,
you shall have a pure body.
If you have a gracious guru,
you shall repeat His Name.

If you have a gracious guru,
you shall grasp the three worlds.
If you have a gracious guru,
you shall perceive the highest stage.
If you have a gracious guru,
your head shall touch the sky.

If you have a gracious guru,
you shall always be complimented.

If you have a gracious guru,
you shall forsake the world.
If you have a gracious guru,
you shall eschew slander.
If you have a gracious guru,
you shall see good and evil as the same.
If you have a gracious guru,
your fate shall be re-written for the better.

If you have a gracious guru,
your body shall not be overcome with lust.
If you have a gracious guru,
you shall have temples turn for you.
If you have a gracious guru,
you shall have a roof over your head.
If you have a gracious guru,
you shall return the bed.

If you have a gracious guru,
you shall bathe at all the shrines.
If you have a gracious guru,
the discus shall adorn your body.
If you have a gracious guru,
you shall serve the twelve *lingams*.
If you have a gracious guru,
you shall deem poison to be sweet.

If you have a gracious guru,
you shall break all doubts.
If you have a gracious guru,
you shall be free of Yama.
If you have a gracious guru,
you shall swim over the world's ocean.
If you have a gracious guru,
you shall neither be born nor die.

If you have a gracious guru,
you shall find the *Puranas* useless.
If you have a gracious guru,

you shall possess all things that grow.
Without a gracious guru
there can be no resting place.
Therefore Namdeva
seeks the guru's refuge.

12.

Come, O *qalandar* Keshava,
You who wear the garb
of an *Abdali* fakir. (Rest)

You have made the sky a peaked cap
for your head, and the nether-worlds
are clogs for your feet.
All skin-bearing creatures
are Your houses of worship.
Such is Your garb, O Gopal.

The fifty-six million clouds
are Your robe,
and the sixteen thousand worlds
are Your waistband.
All the world's flora is your staff,
and the earth is Your platter.

The body is the mosque,
the heart its *mullah*
who perpetually utters
hidden prayers.
You are married to Lady Kamla,
O all-pervasive Nirankar.

As I sang, You let them
take away my cymbals.
To whom should I call out?
Namdeva's Lord
is the Searcher of hearts
who wanders through all the lands.

Raga Basant

1.

If a master be harsh,
the servant runs off,
but he doesn't survive long,
and the families of both
are put to shame.

I shall not forsake Your worship,
though people laugh.
Your lotus feet
ever rest upon my heart. (Rest)

Like a man will gamble his life
for his wealth—
thus saintly people
cannot let go of Ram's Name.

Going off to the Ganges,
or to Gaya, or even to Godavari
means nothing at all.
May Namdeva's service please Narayana.

2.

Waves of lust crash and roar
like a river's torrents.
O Keshava,
my body is drowning.

O Gobind, let me swim
across this ocean of the world.
Carry me over,
O father Bithal. (Rest)

My raft is blasted by the wind,
and I cannot steer or row.
How can I cross over to You,
O Bithal?

Have mercy, and show me a trusty guru
who shall act as my guide,
and lead me across,
O Keshava.

Namdeva says,
I don't know how to swim.
Give me Your arm, Your arm,
O my Bithal.

3.

Slowly moves the cart
piled high with dirty laundry.
The launderer's wife follows behind,
carrying a washing staff.

Slowly, she takes the cart
to the water tank,
and there the dear woman
begins the washing. (Rest)

The launderer, dyed with love,
scrubs and rinses.
How his heart
is fixed upon Hari's feet.

Namdeva says,
He is all-pervasive.
O Lord,
have mercy on Your follower.

Raga Sarang

1.

Why, O my brother,
has your heart wandered into
the forest of Maya?
In confusion you have eaten
the benumbing fruit,
O my brother. (Rest)

As a fish lives in water
and is unaware of the deadly net.
For the sake of its stomach
it takes the bait—
thus is your love
for gold and women.

As the honey-bee fills the comb,
but a man comes and takes the honey,
leaving only smoke for the bee.
As a cow saves all her milk for her calf—
but the milkman ties her up
and takes everything.

A man will work hard for money,
and then he takes that money
and buries it in the earth—
but the fool does not understand
that the money will remain buried,
while his own body becomes dust.

You burn ceaselessly
with lust, wrath, greed,
you never sit among saintly men.
Namdeva says,
Seek out His protection—
become fearless and praise Bhagvan.

2.

Why don't you gamble with me,
O Madho?
The Lord with His servant,
the servant with His Lord:
such is the game we shall play. (Rest)

You are the god, You are the temple,
You Yourself lead the worship.
Wave upon water, water within wave:
The difference is only
in our speaking and hearing.

You are the singer, You the dancer,
and You Yourself the musician.
Namdeva says, You are my Master.
Your slave is imperfect,
but You are perfect.

3.

The loyal, loving slave
is My very own image.
Even a brief glimpse of him
will allay the three pains,
and draw men out of the world's well. (Rest)

A disciple may loosen
what I have bound,
but what My disciple binds
I cannot loosen.
If he takes and binds Me,
even for an instance,
I cannot protest.

I am bound
by My disciple's merits,
and I am the Life of the world;
yet My slave is My life.
Namdeva, Those who have such a soul,
upon them shines
My own light of love.

Raga Malar

1.

I serve the sovereign Gopal,
the inviolable Niranjan.
Give me the gift of love,
the desire of all saintly men. (Rest)

His house stretches
across the four directions,
and heaven is His mansion and hall.
All the seven regions
He pervades completely.
In His house lives
the ever-youthful Lakshmi,
and the moon and the sun
are His lamps.
Death, that ever looms
over all of mankind,
is a mere play-thing in His court.
Such is the splendor
of the sovereign Lord, Master of men.

In His house,
the four-faced Brahma,
who fashioned all the earth,
is a mere potter.
In His house,
ecstatic Ishvar, the world's guru,
merely preaches
the reality of all things.
Sin and Purity are guards at His door,
and Chitra and Gupta are mere scribes.
Dharamraja, the doom-bringer,
is a mere watchman.
Such is the splendor
of the sovereign Lord, Gopal.

In His house are Shiva's hosts,
celestial singers and sages,
all of whom sing
like poor minstrels.
The *Shastras* are all actors before Him,
and the world is a little stage.
Great kings are His liegemen,
who speak sweet words of praise.
The four winds His fans,
and the all-enticing Maya His slave.
Hell—that sherd of creation is His oven.
Such is the splendor
of the sovereign Lord,
Master of the three worlds.

In His house, Kurma is His bed,
and thousand-hooded Vasuki the mattress.
All vegetation is His flower-girl,
and ninety-six million clouds
are His water-bearers.
Ganges, the stream of the gods,
is the sweat of His brow.
The seven seas
are His overflowing jugs of water.
All living things
are His vessels.
Such is the splendor
of the sovereign Lord,
Sustainer of the three worlds.

In His house
Arjuna, Dhruva, Prahlada, Ambarika
are mere chamberlains.
Before Him sport
Narada, Nejaya, the Siddhas,
the Buddhas, Shiva's hosts,
and the fifty-two heroes.
In His house are a countless number
of living beings,
and in all of them, is He,
the Lord Hari, suffused.
Namdeva says,

I seek His protection,
whose emblem all devotees carry.

2.

Do not forget me,
do not forget me,
do not forget me,
O my precious Ram. (Rest)

I infuriated all those
deluded by their high birth.
With shouts of "Shudra, Shudra,"
they beat me and threw me out.
What am I to do,
O father Bithal?

If You save me only after I die,
no one will know
that I was saved.
These pundits say
I am low caste:
Your very honor
is now at stake.

You, whom we all call
Merciful, Compassionate,
are infinitely strong of arm:
You turned the temple
towards Namdeva,
so that all the pundits sat outside.

Raga Kahanra

Such is the nature of Raja Ram
that He pervades all things—
like seeing one's face
in a mirror. (Rest)

He dwells in every body, every pore;
His mark cannot remain hidden,
yet He Himself is unstained,
nor has He any lineage.

Like seeing one's face
in a pool of water—
such is Namdeva's Master,
the Lord Bithal.

Raga Parbhati

1.

The heart alone
can know its own pain,
which we take
before the Knower
of all things.
I praise Ram,
the Searcher of hearts.
Why should I be afraid?

Gopal my Master
has threaded me:
my Prabhu is suffused
in all things. (Rest)

In the heart is His workshop,
in the heart is His city,
and in the heart
is He the artisan.
In the heart dwells
the Creator of all forms,
and all shapes and colors.
The world walks on in error.

The Word of the guru
soaks the heart,
and doubt vanishes.
Then we come
to dwell in the Infinite.
All things obey His decree.
Fearlessly we must accept
that all creatures are equal.

The soul that perceives this
praises Purushotama

and utters words
of the highest wisdom.
Namdeva says,
I have found the Life of the world:
in my own heart lives
the uninscribable One.

2.

From the beginning of time,
eternal, from age to age,
was He who knows no end.
Inside each one of us
is blended Ram.
Thus does He show Himself.

Gobind thunders,
the Word resounds.
My beautiful Ram
is the very face of bliss. (Rest)

The sandal-tree within a forest
gives its pleasant perfume to all.
He is the Essence
of all fragrances:
even common wood
becomes fragrant with His touch.

You are the philosopher's stone,
and I am iron.
By Your touch
I am changed to gold.
You are the jewel, the ruby of mercy:
Namdeva is now blended with Truth.

3.

The Being without lineage
staged a play—
hiding Brahma
in every pore and body.

None can say whence emerges
the Light of life.
Yet He knows all
that you or I do. (Rest)

Like a pot emerges
from shapeless clay—
such is the creation
of the Lord Bithal.

Karma is the snare
of the soul.
Yet all that we do
is His doing.

Namdeva says, The soul acquires
what it longs for—
becoming immortal,
being without lineage.

RAVI DASS

The forty hymns of Ravi Dass preserved in The Adi Granth provide us with the essentials of his biography, which can only be skeletal at best.

He lived in Benares (Varanasi) and was a tanner and cobbler by caste. As such he occupied the lowest rungs of Hindu society, given the extreme miasma associated with touching dead animals. Ravi Dass himself tells us that he and his family daily removed dead cattle from Benares. Like Namdeva and Kabir, both of whom he mentions in his songs, Ravi Dass carried on his trade while preaching his message through song.

Hagiographic accounts say that Ravi Dass (along with Kabir, Pipa, Sain, and Dhanna) was the disciple of Ramananda, the first proponent of bhakti in northern India. It is only because of this fact that we can historically contextualize Ravi Dass and deduce that he lived sometime during the fifteenth century.

The language of these forty songs is largely santbhasha, with elements of Old Hindi—a dialect very similar to the one used by Kabir in The Adi Granth recension.

THE SONGS OF RAVI DASS

Sri Raga

You and I,
I and You—
how are we different?
Only in the sense
that gold
differs from the bracelet,
and water
differs from the wave.

If I did not sin,
O eternal Lord,
You could not be called
Purifier of sin. (Rest)

It is You
who is the Savior,
the Searcher of hearts.
A master may be known
through his servants,
and the servant
may be known
through his master.

Grant me
that I may adore You
so long as my body
does not perish.
O Ravi Dass,
only a very few
can understand
Him who pervades all creation.

Raga Gauri-Guareri

1.

I keep company with the low,
and day and night I worry:
my Karma is evil,
and I am low-born.

O my Ram, my Gosain,
Life of my life.
Do not forget me.
I am Your slave. (Rest)

Take away my worry,
and make me pure.
I shall not leave Your feet
though my body perish.

Ravi Dass says,
I am at Your mercy.
Come quickly to Your slave.
Do not delay longer.

2.

There is a city called Sorrowfree,
where suffering and pain cannot enter.
No anxiety is found there,
nor wealth,
nor anyone to tax it.
Fear of sin and dread of death
do not live there.

I have found a wonderful place,
where I can be happy, O brothers. (Rest)

Strong and eternal
is the kingship there.
There are no ranks;
all are equally treated.
Flourishing and famous is that city,
whose citizens
have all they need.

They all stroll about
where they please,
no one hinders them.
The emancipated cobbler
Ravi Dass says,
All my fellow-citizens there
are also my friends.

Raga Gauri-Bairagan

Steep is the road, sheer the drops,
and I have only a useless ox.
My sole prayer
to my beloved Ram is this:
keep my few belongings safe,
O Murari.

Is there any other merchant for Ram?
My load is almost full. (Rest)

I am a merchant for Ram,
and I deal in eternity.
My full load
is Ram's name.
The world's load
is all poison.

O angels who see this world
and the next,
write down what you will of me.
Yama's staff will not strike me,
nor shall shackles
hold me fast.

This world
is like the color
of safflower.
The dye of my beautiful Ram
is like that of madder,
thus says Ravi Dass the cobbler.

Raga Gauri-Purbi

Like a well filled with frogs
that know nothing of other lands,
so my heart,
rapt with worldly delight,
knows nothing of this world
or the next.

O Lord of all creation,
show Yourself for an instant. (Rest)

My mind is sullied, O Madho;
I cannot grasp the substance
of Your reality.
Have mercy and lift my confusion.
Grant me wisdom
that I may come to understand.

Even great yogis
cannot begin to describe
all Your virtues.
I want to love You
and worship You,
so says Ravi Dass the cobbler.

Raga Gauri-Bairagan

In the *satya-yuga* was truth,
in the *treta-yuga* was sacrifice,
in the *dvapara-yuga* was worship.
It was during these three ages
that these three rites were fixed.
In our own *kali-yuga*,
we have only the Name
as our strength.

O my brother,
how shall we get across?
No one comes and tells me,
how to end my coming and going. (Rest)

There are so many religions,
so many creeds
that people follow and practice
in this world.
How can we break free
from our Karma?
Which religion shall set
all thing right?

We may think and ponder
upon correct rites
and rituals,
and the *Vedas* and the *Puranas*
merely bring on more doubt.
Fear never leaves my heart,
for my ego
remains unconquered.

My body, my outer self,
I wash daily with water,
but my heart,
my inner self,

cannot be cleaned.
How can I make myself pure?
Truly, achieving purity
is work for an elephant.

The sun can vanquish
the murk of the night,
as all the world well knows.
And, in a blink of an eye,
copper can at once
turn into gold
when touched
by the philosopher's stone.

But if, by some great fortune,
I meet the true guru,
who is the best
philosopher's stone,
my soul's innermost desire
shall be fulfilled—
God shall dwell in my heart,
opening wide all rusted-shut doors.

Then shall I know the path of love,
of discipline, of true wisdom,
and the fetters of doubt
shall be cut from me.
With great bliss
shall I meet the in-dwelling Lord—
no difference shall then remain
between virtue and vice.

And yet have I
so often sought
to free myself
from the noose of doubt.
But still devotion and love
do not well up in my heart—
for this reason
is Ravi Dass filled with sorrow.

Raga Asa

1.

Deer, fish, bumble-bees,
moths and elephants—
all perish
because of one vice.
What hope have we
who have five unruly vices?

O Madho, we have loved folly.
Our lamp of wisdom is sooty. (Rest)

The careless are like animals,
who by nature do not know the difference
between sin and purity.
Though they achieve human birth,
so difficult to attain,
yet they remain base.

All creatures exist
according to their Karma.
And the eternal noose of Death
snares them all;
no amount of cunning
can loosen it.

O slave Ravi Dass, forsake fear,
and make the guru's wisdom
your most fervent penance.
You, who breaks
the fear of Your disciples,
grant me eternal bliss.

2.

Holy men are Your body,
their company is Your breath.

By the wisdom of the true guru
I now know
holy men are the gods of gods.

The company of a holy man,
the pleasure of his words.
The love within a holy man—
grant me these things,
O God of gods. (Rest)

The works of a holy man,
the path walked by a holy man,
the service of a holy man
to even the meanest slave—
grant me these things.

Grant me also
the gem of devotion,
and do not lead me
into the sinful company
of the unholy.

Ravi Dass says,
Those who know this are wise:
there is no difference
between a holy man
and God everlasting.

3.

You are a high sandal-tree,
and I am a useless weed
growing beside You.
From a seedling I grew tall,
and now I too am scented
by sweet perfume.

O Madho,
I have sought
Your companionship
as my protection.

I am without merit.
You are forever merciful. (Rest)

You are fine silk,
woven white and yellow.
I am merely a silkworm.
May I ever walk
with holy men, O Madho,
like a bee in a hive.

Low is my caste,
low my lineage,
and low my very birth—
this is so because I did not
serve the Raja Ram,
so says Ravi Dass the cobbler.

4.

What would it matter,
if my body were broken to bits?
Your slave only fears
that love may leave his heart.

Your feet are the lotus,
and my heart is the bumble-bee:
as I drank Your nectar deeply,
I found, I found
the treasure-hoard
of my beloved Ram. (Rest)

Prosperity and misfortune,
riches and wealth—
these are the veils
of Maya herself.
But Your slave
has not lost himself in these.

By the rope of love
is Your slave
bound and tied.

Ravi Dass says,
Where is the virtue
in being free?

5.

Remember Hari, Hari,
Hari, Hari, Hari, Hari.
Even the most unredeemable
were saved
when they remembered Hari. (Rest)

Because of Hari's name
Kabir received fame,
and all the records
of his past lives
were shredded.

By the grace of Hari,
Namdeva gave God
milk to drink.
And so he did not again return
to this world's suffering.

The slave Ravi Dass
is dyed with Ram's color.
By the guru's grace,
he shall not be cast
into hell.

6.

How the clay doll dances:
it sees everything,
speaks so much
and runs all about. (Rest)

When it finds something
it grows very proud.
When riches vanish,
it begins to weep.

Its heart and words
and acts are rapt in pleasure.
Where does it vanish
when it dies?

Ravi Dass says,
The world is a gamble, O brothers,
and I have fallen in love
with the Gambler.

Raga Gujri

Milk is unclean because the calf
first sucked the udders;
the flower was tainted by the bumble-bee,
and water defiled by the fish.

O my mother, what shall I take Gobind
for a pure offering?
No offering can be purer
than flowers. (Rest)

The sandal-tree
is entwined by snakes.
Thus do poison and ambrosia
exist side by side.

Incense and fragrant-oiled lamps
are defiled by our smelling.
With what shall Your slave-girl
worship and adore You?

I shall bring heart and body
as my offerings for worship.
By the guru's grace
I shall obtain Niranjan.

If I cannot come
to worship and adore You,
Ravi Dass says,
What shall be my plight?

Raga Sorath

1.

When I existed,
You did not.
Now You exist
and I do not:
as a storm lifts waves
from water—
still they are water
within water.

O Madho,
how can we describe
this illusion?
What we believe does not exist. (Rest)

A mighty king sleeps
on his throne
and in his dream
becomes a beggar.
Seeing his kingdom vanish
before him
he greatly mourns—
such is our condition.

Like the tale
of the serpent
and the rope—
I know a little
of the secret.
Seeing many bracelets
we think gold has many forms—
but it is always forever gold.

In all things
exists the Lord,

assuming countless shapes;
in each pore he plays and sports.
Ravi Dass say,
He is nearer than my hand.
All that comes to pass
is by His will alone.

2.

When You bound me
with the noose of illusion,
I in turn tied You
with the rope of love.
Now try to get free
if You can.
I freed myself
by adoring You.

O Madho, this is how things stand.
Tell me, what will You do now? (Rest)

Though a fish
is netted,
and gutted,
then sliced
into pieces,
and cooked in so many ways,
still it does not forget
the water.

God is not the birth-right
of the select few,
for Raja Hari
belongs to all those
who love Him.
Though the veil of illusion
cover the entire world,
it cannot cover His disciples.

Say Ravi Dass,
My love for Him has grown.

How can I explain this
to other people?
That pain,
which I begged and prayed
for You to remove,
I still suffer and endure.

3.

This human birth,
so difficult to obtain,
is the fruit
of my good deeds.
But I waste it
in ignorance.
Palaces as grand
as those of Lord Indra
in heaven—
tell me,
what use are they
without love for Hari?

I never thought
of the pleasures
of my Lord Ram—
that can make us forget
all the pleasures
of this world. (Rest)

By my own will
I became a fool
and then became insane.
I passed
the days of my life
thinking good thoughts
as well as bad.
Lust is strong
and true wisdom
is always weak.
I was unaware
of my greatest need.

I say one thing,
and then
do something else.
I cannot understand
the reality
of vastly powerful Maya.
The sorrowing slave
Ravi Dass says,
Drive Your anger
far away,
and have mercy
upon my soul.

4.

O Ocean of Bliss,
You possess
the five heavenly trees,
the wish-fulfilling gem,
and the cow
that grants all wishes.
In Your hand
are the four goals of life,
the eighteen powers,
and the nine treasures.

Repeat
Hari, Hari, Hari
with your tongue,
and forsake
all other
worthless efforts. (Rest)

All those countless stories
and accounts
told in the *Puranas*
and the *Vedas*
are merely a play
of the alphabet.
Vyasa, after meditating,
spoke the truth—

there is nothing higher
than the name of Ram.

The fortunate few
who find His love
abide forever
in the eternal realm.
Say Ravi Dass,
Those who have His light
in their hearts
chase away forever
the fear of dying
and being reborn.

5.

If You are a mountain,
then I am a peacock.
If You are the moon,
then I am a partridge.

O Madho, if You break from me,
then I shall break with You.
And if I break from You,
to whom shall I then go? (Rest)

If You are the lamp,
then I am the wick.
If You are the shrine,
then I am the pilgrim.

My love for You
is true and real.
When I fell in love with You,
I gave up my love for others.

Wherever I go,
there I seek to serve You.
No other god
can be a Master like You.

By praising You,
I cut Yama's noose.
Yearning for love
Ravi Dass loudly sings.

6.

A wall of water,
a pillar of air;
blood and semen
as mortar;
a skeleton-cage
of bone, flesh, veins—
thus the poor bird
lives out its days.

O mortal,
what is yours,
what is mine?
We are like birds
living in a tree. (Rest)

Lay out the walls,
dig the foundations—
but your limit
is only three yards and a half.

Well-groomed hair,
a slanted turban.
The body's beauty
will become a heap of ash.

A high house
and a beautiful woman.
Without Ram's name,
you've lost the game.

Low is my caste,
low my whole lineage,
low my very birth.
I seek Your protection,

O Raja Ram Chandra—
thus says Ravi Dass the cobbler.

7.

I am a poor cobbler
who doesn't even know
how to tie a knot,
and people want me
to mend their shoes. (Rest)

I don't have an awl
to stitch with,
nor a knife
with which
to cut out patches.

Because many were busy
tying knots,
they were lost.
I have obtained my desire
without a single knot.

Ravi Dass
forever repeats
Ram's name.
I have nothing
to do with Yama.

Raga Dhanashri

1.

I am the most wretched,
You are forever merciful.
What more is there left to say?

By speaking of You
I calm my heart.
Grant hope to Your slave.

I give myself as a living sacrifice
to my beloved Ram.
But why does He stay silent? (Rest)

We have been separated
for many lives, O Madho.
But now this life is for You.

Ravi Dass says,
Your hope keeps me alive.
It has been long since I've seen You.

2.

My thoughts are only about You,
my eyes see only You,
my ears hear only
Your enchanting praise.
Make my soul a bumble-bee
and place Your feet in my heart.
Let my tongue forever
repeat Ram's ambrosial name.

May my love for Gobind
never lessen,

for I bought it at a high price—
with the worth of my soul. (Rest)

Without the company of holy men,
love cannot grow inside me.
And without love
how can I serve You?
Ravi Dass begs
one favor from Hari:
safeguard my purity,
O Raja Ram.

3.

Your name is my *arati*,
O my beloved Murari.
Without Hari's name
all is vanity. (Rest)

Your name is my prayer-mat,
Your name is my grater,
Your name the saffron
that I take and sprinkle
before You.
Your name is holy water,
Your name is sandal-wood,
and I grate Your name
by repeating it,
which I then offer to You.

Your name is the lamp,
Your name is the wick,
Your name is the oil
that I pour into the lamp.
Your name is the fire
that lights the lamp,
and the light
from this lamp
glows and illumines
all the three worlds.

Your name is the string,
Your name the garland of flowers,
for all other
flowers and plants
are unclean and impure for You.
What can I offer You,
for You are the Creator
of all that exists.
It is Your name
that I wave over You.

The eighteen *Puranas*,
the sixty-eight shrines,
the four castes—
it is in these things
that the world
has lost itself completely.
Ravi Dass says,
Your name is my *arati*.
Only Your true name
can be a fit offering to You.

Raga Jaitsari

O Lord,
I know nothing at all:
I have sold my heart
into the hands of Maya. (Rest)

You are called
the world's Guide and Master;
they call me
the lecher of this age.

These five
have perverted my heart.
With each passing moment
they led me further away from Hari.

Wherever I look
I see the noose of suffering—
still I don't believe—
all holy books are my witnesses.

Like Gautama's wife,
Oma's lord and master,
the head-holder,
and he who bore a thousand vaginas—

the evil five bound all of them
and beat them shamelessly.
The same five beat me also,
yet wantonly I cling to them still.

Ravi Dass say,
Where shall I go? What shall I do?
Without Raghunath,
whose refuge shall I seek?

Raga Suhi

1.

Only a happy wife
can know her husband's worth:
she forsakes her pride
and embraces him,
and thus reaps great bliss.
She offers him
her heart, soul and body,
holding nothing back.
She does not yearn for another,
nor heeds the follies of her heart.

How can she know
the pain felt by others?
For she has never felt
the pain of separation. (Rest)

The tormented, unhappy wife
is joyful neither at her parents' house
nor in her husband's house—
because in her heart
she didn't love her husband.
The bridge of Sirat
is narrow and treacherous.
She has no companion
for this journey—
she must go alone.

Suffering,
filled with pain,
I come to Your door.
I am so thirsty,
but there is no answer
at Your door.
Say Ravi Dass,

O Prabhu I seek Your refuge.
Do what You think
is best for me.

2.

Each day that dawns,
also passes away.
We must one day all leave.
Nothing lasts forever.
Our companions left,
and we too must leave.
The road may be long,
but Death hangs over our heads.

What, are you still sleeping?
Wake up, you fool.
You think that this world
and this life are true and real? (Rest)

He who gave you life
shall also sustain you.
He keeps a larder
in every pore.
Go and worship Him.
Stop saying "Me" and "Mine."
Every morning
place His name in your heart.

Your life passed,
yet you never prepared
for the journey ahead.
It is now evening,
and the darkness grows.
Ravi Dass says, O ignorant fool,
can't you see this world
is the house of death.

3.

A high mansion,
a great hall,

vast kitchens—
yet you could not spend
even a single moment
inside it.

This body
is like a bundle of grass:
the grass burned
and again mingled with dust. (Rest)

Brothers, relatives,
family and friends—
even all these
will say:
"Quickly,
get him out of here."

The lady of the house,
your dear wife,
who lovingly embraced you,
now runs off
screaming:
"Ghost! Phantom!"

Say Ravi Dass,
Death has looted
the whole world.
I alone escaped
by saying:
"Ram."

Raga Bilaval

1.

Upon seeing poverty
people laugh and jeer,
and such was my plight.
But now I hold the powers
of creation
in the palm of my hand—
all because of Your mercy.

You know I am nothing,
O Ram, Destroyer of fear.
All creatures seek Your refuge,
O Prabhu, Fulfiller of desires. (Rest)

Those who find Your refuge
suffer no more afflictions.
Because of You,
the high and the low—
all have gone across,
escaping from the prison
of this world.

Ravi Dass says,
The tale cannot be told,
so why speak further?
You are what You are.
What metaphor
can I possibly use
to describe You?

2.

If a *saddhu*
or a *vaishnava* holy man

is born in a family,
though his caste
be high or low,
though he be rich or poor—
still the world
shall call him pure-hearted. (Rest)

Though he be a Brahmin,
a *vaishya*, a shudra,
or a *kshatriya*;
though he be a *dom*,
a *chandal*, an infidel,
or have an evil heart—
yet shall he become pure
when he praises Bhagvan.
Thus shall he save himself
and his family.

Blessed will be his village,
and blessed his very dwelling place.
His family will be deemed blessed
by the whole world.
Those who drink the True Ambrosia,
and forsake all other drinks;
those who become drunk
with this True Drink—
they shall destroy
the poison of sin.

Learned pundits
and great warriors,
mighty canopied kings—
none of them can equal
a lover of God.
Like a lotus stays dry
though floating in a pond—
Ravi Dass says,
Such is the existence
of a holy man.

Raga Gaund

1.

Mukand, Mukand
the world keeps repeating.
Without Mukand
the body withers.
That very Mukand
is the Giver of redemption.
That very Mukand
is my mother and father.

Mukand, while living;
Mukand, while dying.
His servants
are forever blissful. (Rest)

Mukand, Mukand
is my very life-breath.
Remembering Mukand
is my fate and destiny.
He serves Mukand
who forsakes the world.
Mukand's treasure
is found by the poorest man.

If Mukand shows His mercy,
then what harm
can the world do to me.
My caste is erased:
I have become His courtier.
It is You, Mukand
who are my Savior,
from age to age.

Wisdom rises within me.
I have become enlightened.

Through His mercy,
He accepts me, an insect,
as His slave.
Ravi Dass says,
My thirst is now quenched.
Remember Mukand, and serve only Him.

2.

Though a man bathe
in the pools
of all sixty-eight shrines;
though a man worship
the twelve *lingams*;
though he dig public wells
and create ponds of fresh water—
but if he reviles others—
all his good works
shall be utterly wasted.

How can he who reviles holy men
gain salvation?
Realize this—
he shall end up in hell. (Rest)

Though a man observe
all lunar and solar eclipses
at Kurukshetra;
though a man offer
his wife, all richly adorned;
though a man listen
to all the *Smritis*
with utmost care—
but if he reviles others
these deeds shall yield no profit.

Though a man offer
countless oblations
to all the idols,
and though he build
far-shining mansions

and donate lands to temples;
though a man neglect himself
and piously care for others—
but if he reviles others,
he shall wander through countless lives.

Why does all the world
revile each man?
Those who revile
indeed deal in evil wares.
After much consideration
Ravi Dass believes
that a man
who reviles holy men
forever remains a sinner
and will end up in hell.

Raga Ramkali

We all read and praise
and hear His name,
but still we never
gain that boundless Love.
How can iron become
the purest of gold
if it does not
come to touch
the philosopher's stone?

O Deva,
the knot of fear
does not loosen.
Lust, anger, Maya,
pride and envy—
these five
gather together
to rob us all. (Rest)

We are all great poets,
high-born pundits, and adept yogis
and wise holy men.
We are all scholars,
men of virtue, great warriors,
and generous alms-givers—
shall we never be free
of these distinctions?

Ravi Dass says,
not everyone can understand.
Many wander about
as if they were madmen.
My pillar of support
is the name of Narayana.
He is my life,
my very breath, my wealth.

Raga Maru

1.

Who else but You
can do what You do,
O my precious Jewel.
You exalt the low,
O my Gosain,
placing a regal umbrella
above their heads. (Rest)

He whose very touch
can defile the world
and render men impure—
upon him You shower Your mercy.
My Gobind
makes the low high,
for He fears no one.

Namdeva, Kabir,
Trilochan, Sadhna, Sain—
all went across
and were saved.
Ravi Dass says,
Listen, O you holy men,
Hari does all things well.

2.

O my brother,
He is
the Ocean of bliss,
who holds in His hand
the five heavenly trees,
the wish-fulfilling gem,
the cow that grants

all earthly desires.
It is He who holds
the four ends,
the eighteen powers,
and the nine treasures.

Why not let your tongue repeat,
Hari, Hari, Hari,
and forsake all other
useless words. (Rest)

All those countless stories
and accounts
told in the *Puranas*
and the *Vedas*
are merely a play
of the alphabet.
Vyasa, after meditating,
spoke the truth—
there is nothing higher
than the name of Ram.

The fortunate few
who find His love
abide forever
in the eternal realm.
Say Ravi Dass,
The slave who has His light
in his heart
chases away forever
the fear of dying
and being reborn.

Raga Kedara

You perform
all the six duties,
and are high-born,
but you do not love Hari
with all your heart,
and you do not speak
of His lotus feet—
then you are no more
than a carrier of corpses.

O my foolish mind,
think of Him
who is beyond thought.
Just think of Valmiki—
how he was exalted,
though low-born,
because he loved Ram. (Rest)

He was a dog-eater,
completely casteless,
a *chandal*—
yet he loved Krishna.
How can the foolish world
render Him proper praise—
He whose splendor
pervades all
the three worlds.

Ajamala, the prostitute,
the hunter, and the elephant—
all of these
went to Hari.
If such worthless,
unredeemable people
could be saved,
why couldn't you be saved,
O Ravi Dass?

Raga Bhairo

You cannot hope
without first seeing—
but all that we see
is perishable.
He who rightly praises
His name—
that yogi shall be freed
from all worldly desires.

He that forsakes all things
and loses himself in Ram
is touched by the philosopher's stone
and doubts no more. (Rest)

A true sage is he
who banishes doubt
from his heart
and blends with the Formless One
who pervades the three worlds.
People do what their hearts desire:
but he who is fearless
becomes Kratar.

The forest blossoms
in order to bear fruit.
The blossom vanishes
so that fruit may appear.
To get enlightenment
people do so many things.
When enlightenment
is attained Karma vanishes.

The wise woman
churns cultured cream
to make butter—so achieve Nirvana
while you are still living.
Ravi Dass speaks

of the highest abandonment:
why do you not praise Ram
with all your heart, O luckless fool?

Raga Basant

You really know
nothing at all,
O my body—
so swollen with pride
when you merely dress finely.
Don't you know
the proud possess nothing
in the end:
above your head
a raven caws.

O my foolish body,
what are you so proud of?
Like a mushroom
sprouting after rain—
just as quickly
shall you vanish. (Rest)

Like a deer
never learns the secret
that the musk
is in his own body—
and he wanders
searching for it all over.
Those who perceive
the body's reality
shall not be set upon
by Yama's henchmen.

You are so proud
of your son
and your wife.
But the Lord
will want a full account
from you.
O soul, you suffer the pain

of all your past deeds.
Afterwards, who shall call you,
"O beloved, O beloved."

Take the refuge of a holy man
and all your sins,
in their millions,
shall be erased.
Ravi Dass say,
He who repeats His name
without end
is no longer concerned
with caste, birth,
or rebirth.

Raga Malar

1.

The people of this city
know very well
that I am a cobbler by caste.
But in my heart
I ponder upon the virtues
of Ram Gobind. (Rest)

If you mix wine
with the water of the Ganges,
O my brother,
holy men shall not drink it.
But wine, or any other water,
cannot remain separate
once it mixes with the Ganges,
O my brother.

The palm-tree
is thought to be impure,
O my brother.
But if you take its leaves
and write the praises
of Bhagvan upon them,
people will worship them
and bow before them in adoration.

By caste I cure leather,
and remove dead animals every day
from all the parts of Benares.
And yet now
renowned Brahmins
come before me and bow deeply.
The slave Ravi Dass
ever seeks the refuge of Your name.

2.

Those slaves
who remember Hari
cannot see another
who equals Lakshmi's Lord
Kamlapati.
He is alone, unique,
all-pervasive;
He is suffused
in all living pores,
O my brother. (Rest)

He in whose house
the Word of Bhagvan
was being written,
for whom none other existed—
his caste was that
of an untouchable
calico-printer.
That very Word
was inside Vyasa
and made visible in Sanaka—
the splendor of His name
pervades the seven islands.

He in whose house
they celebrated the *eid* of fasting
and the *eid* of sacrifice
when they slaughtered cows,
O my brother,
and they worshipped
sheikhs, martyrs and *pirs*;
he whose father
observed all these practices—
he, that father's son,
O my brother,
all the world knows as the famous Kabir.

He whose family
is all low-caste,
and who go about

removing dead animals
from Benares,
even today—
before the son of such people—
before Ravi Dass,
the slave of slaves
high-born, strict
and orthodox Brahmins
come and deeply bow down.

3.

With what kind of love
shall I meet my Beloved,
my Lord of life?
By meeting holy men
I found
that supreme state. (Rest)

Where shall I go
to wash my dirty clothes?
When sleep comes
how long shall I sleep?

All that I gathered,
I utterly lost.
My shop of false wares
was soon shut down.

Ravi Dass says,
When my account is taken,
all that I have done
shall be made visible.

JAYADEVA

We cannot know for certain that the author of the two songs ascribed to Jayadeva in The Adi Granth is the same as the Jayadeva of *The Gita Govinda* (Song of the Lord), the great twelfth-century Sanskrit narrative poem that charts the love between Radha and Krishna. However, Sikh tradition has always maintained that both authors are the same.

The author of *The Gita Govinda* was a Brahmin, born in Kenduli, Bengal, who flourished sometime in the latter half of the twelfth-century. He was a great scholar of Sanskrit and a vaishnava by creed. He eventually became the court poet for Lakshman Sain, the last Hindu king of Bengal. It is said that Jayadeva renounced the world and became a wandering ascetic, devoting himself to the worship of God—but Vishnu himself intervened and commanded him to marry. This he did, and through the love he bore his wife, he wrote *The Gita Govinda*. Legend has it that Krishna himself came down from heaven and wrote some of the verses.

Jayadeva's songs in The Adi Granth are in a mixture of Sanskrit and eastern Apabhramsa (a later development Sanskrit).

THE SONGS OF JAYADEVA

Raga Gujri

Primal,
All-pervasive,
Unrivaled,
Unchanging,
First Mover,
Hoard of virtue,
All-powerful,
Beyond creation,
Incomprehensible,
Forever present.

Only Ram's name
can entice the heart.
Repeat this always:
His name is ambrosia,
it is the true reality.
Remember His name
and suffering shall vanish.
Remember His name
and birth, old age, death
shall not touch you. (Rest)

If you wish to defeat
Yama and his hordes,
seek honor,
peace and goodness.
The present,
the past, the future
are all transitory
and fleeting—
only He is everlasting
and infinite.

Forsake
all lusts;
do not look longingly

upon what others
possess and hold—
it is not fitting.
Abandon all evil deeds
and all evil thoughts.
Go and seek the refuge
of Chakradhar.

Experience
for yourself
Hari's love
through holiness,
through right deeds,
through right words.
What use is yoga?
What good is the world?
What good is giving alms,
what good penance?

Adore Gobind, Gobind,
O mortal,
for He is the source
of all spiritual power.
Openly, without hesitation,
Jayadeva comes
seeking His refuge—
for He existed in the past,
He exists today.
He abides in all things.

Raga Maru

I drew up breath
through my left nostril,
fixed it
at the bridge of my nose,
and then forced
out that breath
through the right nostril,
while repeating "Om"
sixteen times.
I broke the strength
of my weak heart,
steadied my inconstant spirit,
and gave form
to my inchoate mind—
thus did I drink ambrosia.

O my heart,
sing the praises
of God the primal—
thus shall you lessen
the difference
between you and Him. (Rest)

I worshiped
the Worshipful,
and trusted
the Trustworthy—
like water
can easily blend
with water.
Jayadeva says,
I praised
the victorious Deva,
and found that Brahma
who Himself has no desires,

who is lost forever
in the vastness
of His own self.

TRILOCHAN

Trilochan was a contemporary of Namdeva and was born at Barsi in the Sholapur District of Maharashtra. He was a vaishya by caste and was born sometime in the latter half of the thirteenth century. Very little is known about him otherwise.

The language of these songs is mostly santbhasha, with traces of Gujrati and Marathi.

These hymns advocate the worship of God through the aid of a human guru. In accord with Sikh piety, overt dogmatism is rejected in favor of an inner holiness, reflecting God's presence in the heart.

THE SONGS OF TRILOCHAN

Sri Raga

O mortal, how great
is your love for Maya
that you have even forgotten
old age and death.
You bloom like the lotus
when you behold your family.
Can't you see,
you're living
in a borrowed house,
O foolish man?

The hosts of Yama
come running:
I am nothing before them,
I cannot fight them off.
Few and far between
are the friends
who will come and say:
"Come, my Bithal,
throw Your arms around me.
Come, my Ram, rescue me." (Rest)

Endless and delicious
are the pleasures of this earth;
and these have made you forget,
O mortal.
In this sea of life
you deem yourself deathless.
Blinded by Maya,
you have forgotten how to think—
thus you lost your life,
O worthless fool.

Soon you shall have to walk
that pitch black path,
O mortal,

where the sun and moon
cannot shine.
You shall lose
Maya's love
only when you
abandon and forsake
this world.

This very day was my soul enlightened
and I beheld Dharamraja:
before him, his hosts struck down
with their hands the mightiest of men.
I was nothing before them.
When I was taught to perceive,
I beheld Narayana in forests and glades.
But You know all things,
O my beloved Ram—
thus speaks Trilochan.

Raga Gujri

1.

You never purified
the filth inside you,
yet outside you wear
the clothes of a holy man.
In the lotus of your heart,
that beats inside your very body,
you never perceived Brahma.
Say, why do you call yourself
a saintly ascetic?

The world is lost
in forgetfulness,
O Jaya Chandra:
never, never
does it perceive
Parmananda. (Rest)

Eating from house to house,
you fatten your body:
your patched coat and earrings
are all for Maya.
You smear yourself with ashes
from cremation grounds—
yet without a guru,
you never discerned
the true essence of all things.

O mortal,
why do you worship?
Why do you pray?
Why churn water for butter?
He who created the circle
of eight million,
four hundred thousand lives—

Him you should remember,
for He is free of all care.

O holy man,
why do you carry
a wooden bowl with you,
and wander through all
the sixty-eight shrines?
Trilochan will only say this:
if you haven't any grain,
O mortal,
why go to the threshing?

2.

In the final hour,
he who thinks of wealth,
and dies with only this in mind,
shall be born a serpent,
again and again.

O my sister,
forget not Gobind's name. (Rest)

In the final hour,
he who thinks of women
and dies with only this in mind,
shall be born a whore,
again and again.

In the final hour,
he who thinks of boys
and dies with only this in mind,
shall be born a hog,
again and again.

In the final hour,
he who thinks of houses
and dies with only this in mind,
shall be born a demon,
again and again.

In the final hour,
he who thinks of Narayana
and dies with only this in mind,
shall be saved, says Trilochan,
for Pitamber is in his heart.

Raga Dhanashri

Why curse Narayana,
O foolish, lost woman?
Sorrow and happiness
are the fruits
of your Karma,
O woman. (Rest)

The moon adorns
the brow of Shiva,
and daily it dips
into the Ganges,
O woman,
from where sprang Sarangdhar—
yet it did not lose
its stain—
the fruit of past misdeeds,
O woman.

Aruna, the charioteer
of the lord who is
the lamp of all the world,
and the brother of Garuda,
the king of all the birds,
is himself lame,
because of past misdeeds,
O woman.

The Breaker of sin,
the Lord of all the three worlds,
wandered around,
from shrine to shrine,
O woman,
yet still he was not
cleansed of sin,
and could not let go
of Brahma's head,
O woman.

The World Ocean,
the lord of all rivers and seas,
from whom arose ambrosia,
the moon, the cow Kamdhenu,
Lakshmi, the magical tree,
the high-eared, seven-headed horse,
the all-wise physician—
is forever brackish
because of past misdeeds,
O woman.

Hanumana burnt down the city of Lanka
and dug up the forest of Ravana,
and he gladdened Hari's heart
by finding and bringing
the herb that destroys all pain—
yet he himself took away
nothing more than the little loincloth
that he always wore,
because of past misdeeds,
O woman.

Past deeds
cannot be erased,
O lady of my house,
this is why
I forever repeat
Ram's name.
Thus it is
that Trilochan
himself says,
O my beloved Ram.

BENI

Nothing is known about Beni, except that his language points to a rather early date, perhaps the late thirteenth or early fourteenth centuries. The message in these songs largely affirms the Sikh creed of strict monotheism.

The language of these songs itself is santbhasha, with the exception of the song in *Raga Parbhati*, which is in Sahaskrit, a scholarly language that combines Prakrit, Sanskrit, and Hindi.

THE SONGS OF BENI

Sri Raga

(To be sung like *Paharia*)

O man,
when you hung upside down
in the girth of the womb
your mind was ever fixed
upon the High One.
You were not proud
of your body of clay;
day and night your thoughts
were upon the One,
for ignorance was not inside you.
Remember those days:
the hardship, the great suffering.
But now your mind
is lost in so many things.
You left the womb
and entered the circle of death,
and drove the Lord of men
from your thoughts.

O fool,
later you shall be filled
with regret.
What folly, what evil counsel
are you following?
Remember Ram,
so that you may not be pushed
into the city of Yama
like a lost soul. (Rest)

As a child,
your mind was filled with games
and with little delights.
Thus you learned
to love the world.

For the sake of pleasure
you drank poison
deeming it holy ambrosia.
Thus were you tortured
by the five senses.
Worship, penance,
abstinence, holy wisdom—
these you abandoned,
nor did you worship Ram's name.
Driven by lust,
your mind became a darkness,
and all you could do
was go and embrace a woman.

In the ardor of youth
you looked only
upon the faces of women;
you could not discern
the good season from bad.
You were drunk with lust,
swimming in poison,
and you did not know
good from evil.
Seeing your sons and your wealth,
your soul swelled with pride,
and you lost Ram
from your heart.
When others died,
you measured your gain.
Thus did you lose
your beautiful,
luck-filled life.

Your hair is now whiter
than jasmine flowers,
and your words sound
as if they are coming
from the seventh nether region.
Your eyes ever leak,
and your senses and strength
have completely vanished.
Yet lust still churns

within your breast
and passions rain
upon your heart,
though your body has withered
like the lotus.
In this circle of death
you forsook
all words of worship—
thus now are you full of regrets.

Seeing your grandsons
your heart surges
with great love—
pride still blinds you.
You long for a longer life,
though your eyes
can see nothing.
Soon your strength wanes,
and your soul
flies off like a bird.
Now no one wants you
either inside
your own house
or outside it.
Beni says,
Listen, O you holy men,
who can obtain salvation
after death?

Raga Ramkali

The *ira*-vein,
the *pingala*-vein,
the *sukhmana*-vein—
these three
converge at one spot.
Where the three rivers meet,
there is found holy Prayag—
and it is there
that the heart bathes
and becomes clean.

O you saints,
it is there that you find
the faultless Ram.
Only the fortunate few
who follow the guru's path
understand this truth:
the eternal Ram
is forever blended therein. (Rest)

What are the manifestations
of Deva's abode?
There,
resounds the Word unspoken.
There,
neither moon nor sun,
air nor water exist.
Those who follow
the guru's words
know all this already.

Divine wisdom awakens
and hard-heartedness
melts away;
sweet ambrosia
soaks and wets

the inner sky.
Those who know the secret
of this discipline
will surely meet
the primal Gurudeva.

Beyond the Tenth Door
is the abode
of the inaccessible,
the unfathomable
Primal Being.
Above the body,
upon the body
is an alcove.
Within this alcove
is His abode.

Be vigilant;
do not fall asleep.
Attain that stage
wherein the three qualities
and the three worlds
count for nothing.
Place the seed-mantra
within your heart.
Turn back your mind
and fix it upon Silence.

Be vigilant;
do not dwell in falsehood.
Restrain and hold back
the five senses.
Place the guru's teaching
in your thoughts,
and lay your body
and your soul
as an offering
to Krishna's love.

Deem your hands and fingers
as branches of a tree:
do not lose your life

as in a gambling match.
Well up the spring that feeds
the stream of evil deeds;
drive the sun away from the west.
Restrain what cannot be restrained,
and let the spring gush forth:
thus converse with Jaganath.

A lamp
with four wicks
illumines the Tenth Door:
countless petals surround
the flower's cup.
Therein dwells
the Lord Himself,
holding all His power:
a ruby hidden
by another precious ruby.

In the brain
is the lotus
encircled by diamonds.
Therein is Niranjan,
the Holder
of the three worlds.
All the five types of instruments
play sweetly on;
the fan sways;
the conch forever resounds.

The guru's enlightenment
tramples all demons underfoot:
Beni begs for Your name.

Raga Parbhati

You smear sandal-paste
upon your body,
and you put basil leaves
upon your forehead.
But in your heart,
in your hands
you carry sharp scissors.
You look around you
like a thug,
intent as a crane
upon its prey.
You seem like a *vaishnava*
a holy man,
but you have no life-breath
inside you.

You are forever
bowing to your idol,
but you have an evil eye.
At night you lose yourself
in carnal delights. (Rest)

You are forever
bathing and cleaning
your body,
and you change clothes
twice a day.
Your lips touch
only milk
according to a holy vow
you have taken.
But inside your heart
you have a poised knife,
ready to strike;
and it is your habit
to steal money
from all and sundry.

You sit and worship
a stone,
and on your body
you draw circles
in honor of Ganesha.
You stay awake
all night long,
pretending to carry out
pious devotions.
Your feet dance
for the gods
but your mind
is pondering evil.
O sinner, you do not dance
out of piety.

You sit
upon a fawnskin
and hold
a basil-wood rosary;
with hands
ritually cleansed
you daub your forehead
with a gaudy, holy mark.
In your heart
is utter filth,
but around your neck hangs
a *rudrakhan* necklace.
O sinner,
you never repeat
the name of Krishna.

The man
who has not perceived
the reality of God
is blind
and practices
and follows
an empty religion.
Beni says:
become one
with the guru

and follow
his teaching.
Without the True Guru
you shall never
find the true path.

RAMANANDA

Ramananda is the famous bhakti reformer of northern India, who was the disciple of Ramanuja, the equally renowned teacher of vaishnava principles. Both men were Brahmins by caste. Ramanuja's concept of bhakti stressed precise observance of ritualistic and caste duties and largely underplayed love of the individual for God. He gave Brahminism a new justification by merging it with a devotional way of life.

His disciple, Ramananda, largely accepted this version of bhakti while at the same time radicalizing it—in that he accepted disciples from the lower castes; traditionally, religious precepts were the preserve of the higher castes only. But this acceptance of inferior castes did not mean equality: each person had to perform the obligatory duties of his caste, so he could rise through the castes, by way of rebirth, and eventually be born a Brahmin—only then could that person be a true vaishnava devotee. However, Ramananda's concept of bhakti did serve to abolish the concept of pollution associated with the lower castes for he enjoined his followers to eat together; however, the caste system itself remained a valid and necessary component for Ramananda. In traditional Indian society, a member of the first three castes would never eat or associate with the lower castes for fear of ritual pollution.

Ramananda's exact dates are not known, but he probably flourished from the latter part of the fourteenth century to the middle of the fifteenth. His disciples included such famous saints as Kabir, Ravi Dass, Pipa, Sadhna, and Sain.

Only one of his songs survives and that is preserved in The Adi Granth. This song propounds monotheism, under the guidance of a guru, and suggests that true worship is a personal devotion to the Divine. The language of the song is Braj, from the northeast sector of the greater Hindi belt.

THE SONG OF RAMANANDA

Raga Basant

O my brother,
Where shall I go,
why should I wander?
The pleasure I seek
is in my very own home.
My mind will not stray,
for my heart
is now steadfast. (Rest)

One day,
a yearning arose in my heart,
and I went with
sandal shavings and essence
and so many perfumes,
so I could worship Brahma
in the temple.
But then the guru told me
that the Brahma I sought
dwelt in my very own heart.

Wherever I went
I met only water and stone—
but You remain
all-pervasive
and forever unchanging.
I read and searched
all the *Vedas*
and the *Puranas*;
I go to them
if I do not find Him here.

O my true guru,
I am your handmaid,
your living sacrifice,
for you have cut away
all my hardened doubts,

all my great fears.
Ramananda's Lord
is the all-pervasive Brahma—
a guru's word
can destroy a million sins.

SAIN

Sain lived sometime during the end of the fourteenth century or the beginning of the fifteenth. He was a barber by caste, and tradition holds that he was a disciple of Ramananda. He was in the employ of Raja Ram, king of Rewa, which lies southwest of Benares (Varanasi). Nothing more is known about him.

In Indian society, barbers, though low-caste, play an important function. They arrange weddings, supervise the preparation of feasts, act as surgeons, work as go-betweens for lovers, perform as court-jesters, storytellers, and singers of bardic songs—besides being adept at their own trade.

The language of the single hymn attributed to Sain in The Adi Granth is entirely santbhasha.

THE SONG OF SAIN

Raga Dhanashri

Incense, lamp, clarified butter;
these I gather for my *arati*;
these are my offerings to You,
O Kamlapati.

I am in bliss, I am in bliss
O my Lord Hari.
This bliss is a gift
of my precious Raja Ram. (Rest)

A well-wrought lamp,
the purest wick—
such are You,
O Niranjan, O Kamlapati.

Only a lover of Ram
can know the bliss of Ram;
only a lover can describe
this primal, perfect Bliss.

O alluring One,
O Destroyer of fear, O Gobind.
Sain says,
Praise the supreme Bliss.

DHANNA

Dhanna was a farmer from Rajasthan, and belonged to the Jat caste, whose members are mostly agriculturists. He was reputedly born in 1415 in the village of Dhuan, close to Deoli, and was a disciple of Ramananda.

The Jats are often assumed to be later Aryan settlers in India (although some see them as the nomadic Scythians, because their name resembles the term *Getae*, i.e., Scythians who inhabited the Oxus region). The Jats themselves claim descent from the Yadavas, the tribe to which Krishna belonged. The bulk of the Sikh converts came from the Jat clans in the Panjab.

Legend maintains that as a child, Dhanna was much given to praising God, and his practice evolved from idol worship to strict monotheism, which would explain his inclusion in The Adi Granth. The language he employs is santbhasha.

THE SONGS OF DHANNA

Raga Asa

1.

Many births pass,
lost and wandering:
the body, the self, wealth
do not last forever.
Poisoned by greed,
stained by lust,
the heart forgets
Hari the diamond. (Rest)

The poisoned fruit
you find most sweet,
O foolish heart.
You cannot know
the beauty of contemplation.
Forsaking virtue
you pursue so many other pleasures,
and once more
you erect the loom
of birth and death.

You never established
the true scheme of life
within your heart.
Burning with desires
you were caught
in the noose of Yama.
You gathered and gorged yourself
with so many poisoned fruits
that your heart forgot
Prabhu, the Primal Being.

The guru gives out
the treasure
of inner enlightenment;

only then can you believe
that your heart
has become one with the Lord.
Only love and devotion
can bring you peace,
for you are fully satisfied
and have gained salvation.

Those
in whose hearts
shines
divine light—
they perceive
Prabhu the faultless.
Dhanna found Dharnidhar
as his treasure:
by mingling with saints
he lost himself.

2.
(By Guru Arjan Dev)

To Gobind, Gobind, Gobind
Namdeva lost his heart:
thus a two-bit calico-printer
became worth a million. (Rest)

Leaving his weaving and threading,
Kabir placed his love at His feet:
thus a low-born weaver
became a hoard of virtue.

Ravi Dass forever dragged off dead cows;
and then he forsook Maya:
he was enlightened in the company of saints,
and he was granted a sight of Hari.

Sain the barber, the drudge,
is now praised in every house:
in his heart Parbrahma came to dwell,
and he is now counted among saints.

Hearing such examples,
a poor Jat took up devotion:
I met Gosain in person;
great is Dhanna's fortune.

3.

O mind,
ponder Damodar the merciful.
Do not seek knowledge
of any other,
or you shall wander about
through all of creation:
that which He ordains
comes to pass. (Rest)

Within the waters
of a mother's womb
he places the body
with its ten doors.
He nourishes it,
protects it
in the fiery pit—
such is my Master.

A turtle lives in water,
yet its body is born on land;
it has no wings,
nor does it suckle milk.
But it is complete
in the immutable, blissful Manohar.
Look upon this, O my heart,
and comprehend.

An insect lives
secreted in a stone;
it has no way out.
Dhanna says,
The immutable Lord
belongs even to the insect.
Why, O my soul,
do you fear?

Raga Dhanashri

O Gopal, I am your wretched beggar.
You do all things
for those that love You. (Rest)

Lentils, flour, butter—
these things I beg for.
Make my heart joyful
and grant these goods.
Shoes and some good clothes,
and grain grown
on a well-plowed field.

A milk-cow and a buffalo—
these things I beg for.
A fine mare
from Turkistan,
a good woman for my home—
all these things
Dhanna begs from You.

SADHNA

Sadhna was a butcher by profession; he was born at Sehwan in the Sindh. He was probably a contemporary of Namdeva. It is said that Sadhna abandoned the world in order to pursue his love for God unhindered. According to legend, Sadhna's hands were cut off when he was falsely accused by a woman of killing her husband and trying to rape her. In fact it was she who had murdered her husband so that she could live with Sadhna, so taken was she by his physical beauty. Though falsely accused and punished, Sadhna continued praising God, and soon enough a new pair of hands sprouted from his stumps.

There is a shrine to Sadhna at Sirhind in the Panjab, but as is often the case, precise information about the saint cannot be found. The single song found ascribed to him in The Adi Granth is in santbhasha.

THE SONG OF SADHNA

Raga Bilawal

For a king's daughter,
one man changed his guise;
it was all for lust and desire—
yet You kept his honor.

What good is that virtue,
O Guru of the world,
which cannot destroy Karma?
Why seek a lion's protection
when a jackal can devour me? (Rest)

For one drop of water
the cuckoo suffers so very much.
If it finds an ocean
and yet still lose its life,
where lies the good?

My life tires, begins to ebb away;
how can I teach it patience?
If a boat reaches
a drowned man
how shall he climb in?

I am nothing,
nothing am I,
and I possess nothing.
Now is the time to keep my honor,
for Sadhna is Your slave.

PIPA

Pipa lived during the early part of the fifteenth century and was the king of Gagaraungarh. He was a devotee of the goddess Durga, but for further religious guidance he sought out Ramananda and became his disciple. In time, he forsook his kingdom and throne and became a wandering holy man; his wife Sita accompanied him. Many miracles are attributed to him, and various stories are told of his piety and service to his fellow man.

The single song attributed to him in The Adi Granth points out that the Divine is housed within one's own self, and it is there that one should seek Him. The language of the song is santbhasha.

THE SONG OF PIPA

Raga Dhanashri

The body is God,
the body is the temple,
the body is the worshiper,
the body is the sacred shrine.
The body is the incense,
the lamp, the sacred offerings;
it is the body I worship
with broken petals.

After searching
all the world,
it was in the body
I found all the treasure
of the world.
Nothing is born,
nothing dies—
such is Ram's light. (Rest)

What is contained
in the universe
is also contained
in the body:
whatever you seek,
you shall find.
Pipa says, He is Primal Matter;
the true guru will show this.

SUR DASS

Sur Dass was a Brahmin who lived in the early sixteenth century; he should not be confused with the Sur Dass who wrote the *Sur Sagar*, a cycle of poems that describes Krishna's childhood in Bindraban (Vrindavana).

The Sur Dass of The Adi Granth was a learned man and a skilled musician and poet. He is said to have been appointed governor of Sandila by the emperor Akbar. His shrine can be found in the city of Benares (Varanasi).

There are two hymns in The Adi Granth ascribed to Sur Dass. The first one is only one-line long and the second is a composition by Guru Arjan Dev. We cannot know the reason behind this curious occurrence. Speaking about the line of verse attributed to Sur Dass, Macauliffe says: "The hymn was originally copied into the Granth Sahib of Kartarpur, but a pen was subsequently drawn through it and sulphate of arsenic rubbed over it for complete erasure" (Macauliffe, 1983, Vol. 6:419). However, this statement is contradicted by the fact that the Kartarpur *Adi Granth* (the one compiled by Guru Arjan himself) shows no evidence of such an erasure; there is only the single line of verse, which is then followed by Guru Arjan's song.

As a matter of interest, the Bhai Banno recension of The Adi Granth gives this song in its entirety:

O my heart,
forsake those
who have turned their faces
away from God,
for they merely incite you
to evil passions and desires,
and lead you away
from devotion. (Rest)

Why give milk
to a serpent?
It shall never
be free of its poison.
Why feed costly camphor
to a crow?
Why bathe a dog
in the Ganges?

Why put rare perfume
on a donkey?

Why put precious jewels
on a monkey?
Sinners are like stones:
arrows of divine wisdom
cannot pierce them,
though you shoot a whole quiver.

Sur Dass says,
how can a blanket
made of black wool
be dyed another color?

Perhaps this song was excluded because it portrays a grim picture of sinners who can never be changed. Arjan Dev's song that follows the single line of verse by Sur Dass demonstrates that God can save even the most hardened sinner, if that person perceives and accepts God's reality. Of course, there is strong evidence of doctrinal tampering.

The language of both these songs is santbhasha.

THE SONGS OF SUR DASS

Raga Sarang

1.

O my heart,
forsake those
who have turned their faces
away from God.

2.
(By Guru Arjan Dev)

With God dwell
all God's people.
They offer to Him
their body and soul,
all that they have.
Thus they sway in rapture. (Rest)

Upon beholding Him
all their sins
are washed away,
and they obtain all
they seek
and all they desire.
They crave nothing further,
for they perceive
the alluring, beautiful One.

Those who abandon
the beautiful Shyama
and seek another
are like leeches on a leper.
Sur Dass,
The Lord holds my heart
in His hands;
thus shall He carry me
into the next world.

SHEIKH BHIKHAN

Sheikh Bhikhan was a famous Sufi who lived in the town of Kakori, near Lucknow. He was renowned for his piety and wisdom, and attracted learned men from near and far. He was given the title of sheikh because of his profound understanding of religious matters and principles. He died around 1573.

It is also said that Sheikh Bhikhan was a disciple of Kabir, which may explain the largely Hindu overtones of his two songs in The Adi Granth. The atmosphere of these songs is certainly not Islamic, and the implicit message and salvific process are markedly Hindu. However, there were several Sufis who deliberately confused Muslim and Hindu identities, such as Sheikh Farid, Madho Lal Hussain, and perhaps even Kabir himself.

The language of these two songs is Old Hindi, with few peculiarities of dialect.

THE SONGS OF SHEIKH BHIKHAN

Raga Sorath

1.

Water flows from eyes,
weak is the body,
and hair is white as milk.
The throat, stopped by cough,
cannot utter a single word.
What can a mortal do?

The Lord Ram, Banwari,
shall be my physician:
He forever saves His saints. (Rest)

An ache in the head,
the body burning
as with fire,
pain shooting through the liver.
So great is the malady
that there can be no cure.

Hari's name is pure,
ambrosial water:
there can be no better cure
in all the world.
By the guru's grace, says Bhikhan,
you shall reach salvation's door.

2.

The Name's priceless ruby
I received as my reward
for all my good deeds.
With great cunning and craft
I hid this ruby within my heart,
but it would not stay hidden.

Hari's virtues cannot be described:
like sweets to a mute man. (Rest)

Joyous is my tongue
repeating His name;
joyous my ears
hearing His praise;
joyous my mind
contemplating Him.

Say Bhikhan,
both my eyes are joyous:
wherever I look,
He is there.

PARMANANDA

Parmananda was from Barsi, Maharashtra, the same area as Namdeva; he was a Brahmin by caste. It is difficult to date him; but he probably lived in the early part of the fifteenth century.

He began his religious training as a devotee of Krishna, but as he matured in his religious thinking he became manifestly monotheistic. It is said that he compared himself to a cuckoo (chatrik), which lives on raindrops alone and pines for the monsoons—because he ever burned with the desire to see God and to sing His praises. It is also said that he prayed seven hundred times each day of his life.

His song contains no Marathi, the language of his region, and is entirely santbhasha.

THE SONG OF PARMANANDA

Raga Sarang

O man, what good
is listening to the *Puranas*?
You did not love
with an unceasing love,
nor did you feed the hungry. (Rest)

O Brahmin,
you did not forget lust,
you did not forget anger,
you did not forget greed.
Your mouth did not cease
to utter malicious words:
all your service is fruitless.

By robbing and deceiving others
you filled your belly,
O sinner.
When you go to the next world,
you shall still
be dishonored:
such is the reward
of foolishness.

Your heart
did not give up violence,
and your soul
did not nurture mercy.
O Parmananda,
you did not mingle with saints,
nor did you practice righteousness.

SHEIKH FARID

Sheikh Farid (1173–1266), affectionately known as Baba Farid ("Father Farid"), is the famous Sufi from the Panjab, whose songs and proverbs (in all 134) are second in number only to Kabir (a total of 541) in The Adi Granth. Given Farid's Sufism, his vision fits easily into the broader message of Sikhism, since his emphasis is on God's inviolate oneness. His shrine is at Pak Pattan, Panjab (now in Pakistan).

Farid is also known as Baba Farid *Shakar Ganj* (hoard of sugar); several legends are given to account for this name. The most popular states that when Farid was a child his mother gave him a lump of sugar every time he said his prayers (Muslims are required to pray five times a day). She would place the sugar beneath his prayer rug and say God left it as a reward for his piety. One day, she forgot to leave Farid's reward, and after the child had finished his prayers, he looked beneath his rug, as was his habit, and found a hoard of sugar, left by God this time. More probably, the name derives from the fact that Farid's followers found his words and message sweet, thus bestowing the title upon him.

Macauliffe believes that the verses found in The Adi Granth were written by one Sheikh Brahm, who was also known as Farid *Sani* ("the other Farid"); he was a direct descendent of the first Farid. Sheikh Brahm died in 1552. Certainly, there can be no way to authenticate this idea. It is possible that several "Farids" had a hand in composing the various verses attributed to Baba Farid in The Adi Granth. However, there is one important point that needs to be considered: the language of these songs is a very early form of Panjabi. Thus a case can be made that these songs are by Baba Farid himself, based solely on linguistic evidence.

The language of these songs is pure Lehndi (Western) Panjabi, with some admixture of Persian and santbhasha.

It is important to point out here that Sufism, as it was practiced in the Panjab, stressed concepts that are in harmony with the basic tenants of Sikhism. Thus Sufism propounds a pantheistic point of view, in that God is present in all His creation and can be found immediately in the human heart. The Sufis state that all creatures emanate from God and the final end of all these is a reunion with God. Also, they believe that all religions are one, stemming from the same source, just as the single sun sends out many rays of light, and that all the world's prophets have preached and propounded similar truths: eternal goodness and eternal truth flow from the primal, World-Soul, or God. Further, happiness on earth can be attained by inculcating purity of heart, charity, caring for fellow human beings, self-renunciation, subduing bodily passions, self-control, self-sacrifice, and a profound trust in God.

THE SONGS OF SHEIKH FARID

Raga Asa

1.

True lovers are those
who love with all their hearts.
Those who think of another,
speak of another
are called false lovers.

Those steeped in the color
of God's love
abide in His care.
Those who forget His name
are a burden upon earth. (Rest)

Those whom He gathers
become dervishes at His door.
Exalted are the mothers of such men
who gave them birth,
blessed is their coming into the world.

You are caring, infinite,
boundless, endless.
Those who have discerned
this truth,
their feet, their mouths I kiss.

You are my protection,
O Lord, my salvation.
Grant to Sheikh Farid
the blessing
of Your adoration.

2.

Sheikh Farid speaks:
dear friend, turn to Allah.

This body shall become
dust in the miserable,
dark house of the grave.

Today is the day of union,
O Sheikh Farid,
so tame these wild cranes
of desire that inflame
and incite the heart. (Rest)

We all know that we shall die
and never again return.
Then why do we love
this false world
and sell ourselves?

We must ever speak
of the true path;
let us not speak lies.
Let us walk the guru's course
like humble disciples.

Seeing strong, handsome youths
swim across to the other side,
a weak woman takes heart.
Those who pursue only gold
should be sawn in half.

O Sheikh, no one in this world
can stay alive forever.
The place upon which I now sit,
many have sat before
and gone on their way.

Cranes come in Katak,
forest fires in Chet,
lightning in Savan.
In winter, fair arms of women
adorn lovers' necks.

All ephemeral things pass on.
Think of this, O heart.

That which takes
six months to form
is destroyed in an instant.

The earth asks the sky, O Farid:
how many boatmen have come and gone?
The body merely rots in the grave,
but it is the soul
that must suffer the consequences.

Raga Suhi

Full of anguish
full of sorrow
I writhe and wring my hands:
I need my Beloved!
I am going mad!
My Beloved is angry in His heart.
It is all my wretched fault;
my Beloved is not to blame.

O my Lord,
I did not value Your worth.
Now my youth has withered,
and I am filled with regrets. (Rest)

O black nightingale,
why is it that you are black?
"By the loss of my lover
am I burned.
How can I be happy
without my lover?
If He is merciful,
then Prabhu shall come and meet me."

Frightful is the deep well
and I am a frail girl,
all alone.
I have no companion, no friend.
With Prabhu's mercy,
I joined the company of saints:
and when I looked about me again,
Allah Himself was my friend.

My destined journey
is one of pure sorrow:
sharper than a sword
and keen-edged.

Above it lies my path.
O Sheikh Farid, rise up
and prepare for your pilgrimage
early in the morning.

Raga Suhi-Lalit

When it was time to come to shore
you could not moor your raft.
When the sea tosses and surges,
it is difficult to swim in it.

Do not touch the safflower,
O my dearest friend,
for soon it shall fade away. (Rest)

An ugly wife is often
abused by her husband;
her breasts never give milk.
Never will she know union.

Farid says, Listen O maidens,
when the Husband calls for you,
the reluctant swan is pushed to leave,
and this body becomes a heap of dust.

THE SLOKAS OF SHEIKH FARID

1.

The woman's marriage day
has already been written down.
The lord of whom she only heard about
now comes and shows his face.
He wrenches out her poor life,
cracking all the bones.
Let heart and soul understand
this preordained day cannot be put off.
Life is the bride
that Death the bridegroom
takes away in marriage.
With her own hands she gave herself away.
Whose neck can she now run and embrace?
Have your ears not heard of Sirat Bridge?
O Farid, the call comes.
Stand up, and do not betray yourself.

2.

O Farid, Hard it is
to be a dervish at His door,
for I too walk the way of the world.
I too have a little bundle that I carry.
Where can I go and throw it away?

3.

I know nothing,
I see nothing.
The world is veiled fire.
Gracious was my Sain,
or I too would burned in it.

4.

O Farid, if I had known
there were very few sesame seeds,

I would have filled my hand with great care.
If I had known my bridegroom was a child,
I would have been less vain.

5.

If I had known the skirt
would come apart from the garment,
I would have tied a firmer knot.
I have not seen anyone like You,
though I have traversed this whole earth.

6.

O Farid, if you have
a refined mind,
do not write black words.
Rather, bend your head
and look inside your own self.

7.

O Farid, if people
beat you with their fists,
do not hit them back.
Rather go home,
after kissing their feet.

8.

O Farid, when it was time
to earn some profit,
you were too busy with the world.
Death's foundation got deeper:
what you gathered, you had to lug.

9.

Look, O Farid,
what has come to pass:

your beard has turned white;
what was before, is now near;
what lay behind, is far away.

10.

Look, O Farid,
what has come to pass:
sugar has become poison.
To whom shall I speak my sorrow,
if not to my Sain?

11.

O Farid, my eyes
are weak from seeing,
and my ears deaf from hearing:
the branch has matured
and now shows a different color.

12.

O Farid, those who did not revel
when their hair was dark,
shall not revel when their hair is white.
Love the Lord deeply
and your love shall be ever new.

13.
(By Guru Amar Dass)

O Farid, whether dark-haired or white,
the Lord is unchanging,
if you ponder upon Him.
But this love cannot be gained,
try who might.
The Lord gives His cup of love
to whomever He pleases.

14.

O Farid,
the eyes that loved this world,
those very eyes I have seen:
they could not bear the touch of kohl;
but now young birds nest in them.

15.

O Farid,
I cry, I shout,
I forever give advise.
But those ruined by Satan,
how can their hearts be changed?

16.

O Farid,
become like grass on the road,
if you are seeking the Lord in all things.
Some break you, some trample you:
thus shall you enter the Lord's door.

17.

O Farid,
do not revile dirt,
for nothing is like dirt.
While we live, it is under our feet.
When we die, it lies on top of us.

18.

O Farid,
if you have desires, then where is love?
If you have desires, your love is filth.
How long shall you endure
in a hut collapsing under pouring rain?

19.

O Farid,
why do you wander from forest to forest,
stepping on branches and thorns?
God lives in your very heart.
What are you seeking in a forest?

20.

O Farid,
with these frail legs
I wandered through plains and mountains.
But today, Farid, reaching for this jug
is like walking a hundred-mile road.

21.

O Farid,
the nights are long,
and my back and sides are bed-sore.
How cursed are the lives of those
who have long hopes.

22.

O Farid,
if I keep anything
from a friend,
my body is on fire
like madder burning on coals.

23.

O Farid,
wishing for sweet grapes of Bijaur
the Jat plants acacias;
he spins wool,
while wishing to wear silk.

24.

O Farid,
the path is covered in mire and filth;
the house of my cherished beloved is far.
If I go forward, my cloak shall be ruined;
if I stay my love shall be ruined.

25.

Let my cloak be spattered and ruined;
and let Allah send down more rain.
I shall go and meet my lover
that our love may not break.

26.

O Farid, I am worried
that I may dirty my turban.
But my foolish soul does not realize
that dirt can eat away
even my head.

27.

O Farid, molasses, white sugar,
confectionery, brown sugar,
honey, buffalo-milk—
all these things are sweet.
Yet, Lord, they cannot rival You.

28.

O Farid,
my bread is made of wood,
and hunger is my butter.
Those who eat dainty breads
shall suffer great torment.

29.

Eat dry bread,
and drink cold water.
O Farid, do not look
at the buttered bread of others
and tantalize your heart.

30.

Today I did not sleep
with my Beloved:
my limbs are wracked with pain.
Go and ask the abandoned wife,
how it is that she passes her night.

31.
(By Guru Amar Dass)

There is no room for her
at her in-laws;
nor is she wanted by her parents.
How can the wife
abandoned by her husband be happy?

32.
(By Guru Nanak)

Whether at her in-laws
or at her parents,
she truly belongs to her Husband,
who is unfathomable, unreachable.
Nanak, that wife is truly happy
who loves the One without cares.

33.

Washed, bathed, and adorned—
yet she sleeps carelessly.

O Farid, she is really smeared
with reeking herbs;
all her perfumes are useless.

34.

If I lose my youth, I do not care;
as long as I do not lose my Beloved's love.
O Farid, without love,
the fresh youth of so many,
dried up and shriveled.

35.

O Farid, care is our bed,
pain our mattress,
separation our pillow and sheet.
Such is our life.
Behold, O true Lord, and see.

36.

Separation, separation,
let us all say,
separation you are a great sultan.
O Farid, the body that knows not separation
is barren like a cremation ground.

37.

O Farid,
these are poisonous stalks
smeared with sugar.
Some died planting them,
others perished harvesting them.

38.

O Farid,
twelve hours you lost running around;

the other twelve you lost sleeping.
God will ask you for an account, saying:
"For what reason did you come into the world?"

39.

O Farid,
have you ever gone to court
and seen the gong there?
Though without fault, it is struck often.
What shall become of sinners like me?

40.

Again and again,
it is struck,
beaten hard every hour.
The body is like this gong,
for it too passes the night in pain.

41.

Sheikh Farid has now grown old,
and his body trembles and shakes.
Though one lives to be a hundred,
still the body
shall become dust.

42.

O Farid, sitting at a stranger's door;
Lord, let this not be my fate.
If that is what You have planned for me,
then pull out my life
from my body even now.

43.

An ax on your shoulder,
a water-jug on your head:

O blacksmith, you enter the forest like Caesar.
O Farid, I need my Beloved,
and you need your coal.

44.

O Farid,
some have too much flour,
while others have not even salt.
When they go up ahead,
all shall know who is to be beaten.

45.

They had kettle-drums beating all around
and canopies for their heads;
bards sang their paeans.
But still they went
and slept in cemeteries like orphans.

46.

O Farid, even the builders
of great houses, mansions,
and towered palaces had to leave.
They traded in falsehood
and fell into their graves.

47.

O Farid,
the coat has many patches,
but the soul has never been mended:
turn by turn have departed
so very many sheikhs.

48.

O Farid,
while these two lamps flickered,

the angel of Death came and laid siege.
He ransacked the fort, looted the heart,
and the two lamps went out.

49.

O Farid, look what cotton suffers,
what the sesame seed endures,
the sugarcane, the paper,
the clay-pot, the charcoal.
Evil-doers shall suffer a similar fate.

50.

O Farid, you have
a prayer-rug on your shoulder,
a patched coat on your body:
in your heart you carry a knife,
but your words are sugar-sweet.
From the outside
you seem filled with light—
but inside your heart is black as night.

51.

O Farid,
not a drop of blood would fall,
if someone were to cut my body apart;
for the body steeped in God
no longer contains blood.

52.
(By Guru Amar Dass)

This body is all blood;
no body is without blood.
Those steeped in their Lord
do not have lust in their blood.

When His fear enters, the body weakens,
and lust vanishes from the blood—
just as metal is made pure by fire:
thus fear of Hari banishes hard-heartedness.
Nanak, handsome are the men
who are steeped in Hari's color.

53.

O Farid,
seek out that lake
where you shall find only pure things.
What are you seeking in a pond,
where your hand will plunge only into mud.

54.

O Farid, in her youth
the woman never made love to her Beloved;
then she grew old and died.
Now she calls out from her grave:
"My Beloved, you never came to me."

55.

O Farid, the head is white,
the beard is white,
mustaches too are white.
O foolish, lazy heart,
are you still satisfying lusts?

56.

O Farid, how far can you run on a rooftop?
Banish sleep that separates you
from your Beloved.
The numbered days allotted you
are running away, running away.

57.

O Farid, vaulted houses,
palaces, gabled mansions.
Do not grow fond of them.
When a mound of dirt is thrown on you,
none shall then be your friend.

58.

O Farid,
do not think
of mansions and wealth.
Think of all-powerful Death,
and that place where you are headed.

59.

O Farid,
forsake those evil deeds
that bring no virtue,
so you will not be put to shame
in the court of the Lord.

60.

O Farid,
serve the Master;
banish doubts from your heart.
Dervishes need
the patience of trees.

61.

O Farid,
black are my clothes,
black my attire.
I walk about filled with sin,
but people call me a dervish.

62.

That which is withered
will not blossom
though immersed in water.
O Farid, a cursed woman
ever withers, withers.

63.

A virgin wants to get married;
when she is married,
she is shackled.
O Farid, though she regret her choice,
she cannot again be a virgin.

64.

Upon a brackish pond,
swans come and alight.
They dip their beaks,
but do not drink—
for they long to fly away.

65.

A swan lands upon a field
of coarse grain,
and people rush out to scare him off.
The fools do not know
that swans do not eat coarse grain.

66.

One by one, the birds left
that inhabited this pond.
O Farid, this overflowing pond itself
shall one day dry up;
only the withered lotuses shall remain.

67.

O Farid, a brick shall be your pillow,
you shall sleep in the earth,
and worms shall bite your flesh.
Countless ages shall pass,
but you shall not move.

68.

O Farid,
the beautiful pot has shattered,
and the strong rope has snapped.
In whose house
is the Angel Azrael a guest today?

69.

O Farid,
the beautiful pot has shattered,
and the strong rope has snapped.
Those dear ones who burdened the earth,
how shall they ever return?

70.

O Farid,
you prayerless dog,
what you practice is not good.
You never willingly came
five times to the mosque.

71.

Get up, O Farid,
do your ablutions,
and say the morning prayer.
The head that does not bow to the Lord
shall indeed be cut off.

72.

The head that does not bow to the Lord
what shall we do with it?
We should burn it
beneath a cauldron
in place of firewood.

73.

O Farid,
where are your parents
who gave birth to you?
They have left you long ago,
yet still you do not believe.

74.

O Farid, level the field of your heart;
fill in all the holes.
Thus when you go up ahead,
the fire of hell
shall not loom before you.

75.
(By Guru Arjan Dev)

O Farid, the Lord is in the people,
and the people are in the Lord.
Whom can we call evil,
since there is none but Him?

76.

O Farid, on the day
they cut my umbilical cord,
they should have also cut my throat.
Then I would not have known this suffering,
nor endured all this pain.

77.

Teeth, legs, eyes
and these ears gave up,
and the body
wailed aloud:
"Gone are all my friends."

78.

O Farid,
do good to those who do evil.
Do not let anger wear out your heart.
Thus shall your body be free of taint,
and you shall gain all that you need.

79.

O Farid, this world
is a beautiful garden
in which a bird is a brief guest.
The morning drum now beats.
Get ready. It is time to depart.

80.

O Farid, it was at night
that fragrant musk was shared out.
Those who slept got no share.
What could they get,
for their eyes were filled with sleep.

81.

O Farid, I thought only I suffered;
but the whole world is suffering.
I climbed a high place
and saw that each and every house
burned with the same fire.

82.
(By Guru Arjan Dev)

O Farid,
the world is beautiful;
but in it is a poisonous garden.
Those who are raised high by their *pir*
are not touched by this fire.

83.
(By Guru Arjan Dev)

O Farid,
life is beautiful,
and the body is radiant.
But very few are found
who love the Beloved.

84.

O river, do not break your banks,
for you too must account
for your actions.
Wherever the Lord wills,
there the river must flow.

85.

O Farid,
the day passed in suffering,
and the night passed in torment.
The ferryman stands and calls out:
"The raft is at the lip of the whirlpool."

86.

Long and wide
is the surging river

that eats away its own banks.
What harm can the whirlpool do,
if the ferryman stays alert?

87.

O Farid, many are friends in word alone;
I cannot find one that is true.
But inside, I burn with yearning
for my Friend,
like fire in smoldering ash.

88.

O Farid,
people bark endlessly.
It is hard to endure the clamor.
I shall stop up my ears;
let the wind blow where it will.

89.

O Farid,
God's dates are ripe,
and rivers of honey flow.
Each day that passes
is a hand reaching for my life.

90.

O Farid,
the body dries up, becomes a skeleton,
and ravens peck at my palms.
God still has not come:
behold the plight of Your slave.

91.

Ravens peck my skeleton,
having eaten all the flesh.

O ravens,
do not touch these two eyes,
for they hope yet to see the Beloved.

92.

O ravens,
do not peck my bones;
fly off, if you sit upon them.
The bones in which my Lover dwells,
do not eat their flesh.

93.

O Farid,
the wretched grave cries out:
"O homeless wanderer, come home.
One day you must come to me.
Do not fear Death."

94.

With these two eyes
I have seen so many walk away.
O Farid,
people worry, each for himself.
Just as I worry about myself.

95.

Better yourself, and you shall meet Me.
If you meet Me, you shall be joyous.
O Farid, if you become Mine,
the whole world shall be yours.

96.

How long can a little tree
be hopeful on the bank of a river?

O Farid,
how long can you keep water
in an unfired clay jug?

97.

O Farid, great palaces
became completely empty;
their inhabitants
disappeared into the earth.
Wretched graves lie holding souls.
Say, O Sheikh, worship God;
you must leave,
either today or tomorrow.

98.

O Farid,
Death's boundary is like a river bank.
Beyond it seethe the fires of hell,
from which you hear crying and wailing.
Some have fully understood,
while some others go about
as if without a care.
If you obey Him in this world,
your actions themselves
shall bear witness at His court.

99.

O Farid,
a crane sits
on a river bank and frolics.
The crane, white as a swan,
frolics, and suddenly,
a hawk pounces upon it.
When the hawk of God carries him off,
he forgets all his frolicking.
The things that he never even thought of,
those very things God brought to pass.

100.

A hundred and forty pound body
is set into motion by water and grain.
A man comes into the world
with so many wonderful hopes.
But when the Angel of Death comes,
he breaks down all the doors,
and ties him up
before his own dear brothers.
Behold, a man now walks
on the shoulders of four men.
O Farid, if you obeyed Him in this world,
it will be useful to you at His court.

101.

O Farid, I am a sacrifice to those birds
who live in harsh forests:
they peck at gravel,
live on barren ground,
yet they do not abandon God.

102.

O Farid, the season turns,
the forest trembles,
autumn shakes down leaves.
I have searched all the world over:
nothing lasts forever.

103.

O Farid,
rent your silken veil
and put on a rough, woolen mantle;
wear whatever clothes you must
to meet the Beloved.

104.
(By Guru Amar Dass)

Why rent your silken veil
and put on a rough, woolen blanket?
Nanak, you may meet the Beloved
in your very own home,
as long as your desire is pure.

105.
(By Guru Arjan Dev)

O Farid,
those who were proud of their greatness,
endless wealth and youth,
went to God empty-handed,
like a hilltop after rain.

106.

O Farid, frightening are the faces
of those who have forgotten His name.
Here on earth, they suffer black sorrow,
and up ahead they have
neither house nor home.

107.

O Farid, if you do not wake up
at break of day,
you are dead though alive.
Though you may have forgotten God,
God has not forgotten you.

108.
(By Guru Arjan Dev)

O Farid, the Bridegroom
is exceedingly handsome

and indebted to none.
To be arrayed with Allah's color:
such is true adornment.

109.
(By Guru Arjan Dev)

O Farid,
Suffering and joy are one;
drive out sin from your heart.
What Allah ordains is good:
thus shall you find His court.

110.
(By Guru Arjan Dev)

O Farid, the world sounds
as it is played,
just as you do.
Only that man is not played
whom Allah protects.

111.
(By Guru Arjan Dev)

O Farid, the heart
is enraptured by the world,
though the world is worthless.
Hard it is to follow
the example of fakirs.
To be like them your deeds must be good.

112.

The blossom at the beginning of night
bears fruit at dawn's first light:
those who stay awake
and are vigilant,
obtain their reward from the Lord.

113.

(By Guru Nanak)

Reward is the Master's gift;
none can prevail against Him.
Some, though they stay awake,
get nothing at all.
Some, though asleep, are awakened
to receive their reward.

114.

If you are searching
for the blessed Lord,
then the fault must be yours.
She who is called the blissful bride
does not need to search for another.

115.

Patience within is the bow,
patience is the bowstring,
patience is the arrow,
which the Master
shall not let fall astray.

116.

With inner patience
the patient burn away flesh.
They are close to God,
but they do not give
this secret to others.

117.

Patience is the goal, O mortal.
If you can grasp it,

you shall be a mighty river.
If you break away,
you shall be a little brook.

118.

O Farid,
arduous it is to be a dervish;
even my own love is only skin deep.
Very few follow
the path of the dervish.

119.

The body blazes like an oven,
and bones burn like wood.
Though my feet grow tired,
I shall walk on my hands,
so I could meet my Beloved.

120.
(By Guru Nanak)

Set not your body ablaze like an oven;
do not burn your bones like firewood.
Why walk on your hands or feet,
for the blissful Beloved
is inside you.

121.
(By Guru Ram Dass)

I went searching for my Beloved,
but He was ever with me.
Nanak,
the Unseen is not seen;
only the pious point Him out.

122.
(By Guru Amar Dass)

Seeing swans swim,
the cranes too
were eager to try.
But the poor cranes all drowned,
heads below and feet above.

123.

I thought him to be a great swan,
and so I followed him.
If I had known, he was a wretched crane,
I would not have come near him
all my life long.

124.
(by Guru Nanak)

Swan or crane,
it matters little—
as long as He is gracious.
If He wishes, O Nanak,
He can turn a crow into a swan.

125.

Alone is the bird on the lake;
all around are fifty poachers.
This body is overcome
by high waves. O true Lord,
my hope is in You alone.

126.

What is that word,
what is that virtue,

what the *mantra*,
what garb should I wear
by which I may meet my Beloved?

127.

Humility is that word,
forbearance that virtue,
a kind word that priceless *mantra*.
O sister, take these three as your garb
by which you may meet your Beloved.

128.

Though wise, you are a child;
though strong, you are without strength.
You divide and share with others
when you yourself have nothing:
such are called true saints.

129.

Do not speak a hurtful word,
for in everyone lives the true Lord.
Do not break anyone's heart,
for each heart
is a priceless pearl.

130.

Each heart
is a priceless pearl;
to crush it is evil.
If you wish to meet the Beloved
then do not hurt anyone's heart.

NOTES TO THE SONGS OF THE SAINTS FROM THE ADI GRANTH

NOTES TO THE SONGS OF NAMDEVA

Raga Gauri Cheti:

The story of the "floating stones" comes from the epic *The Ramayana*, which recounts the efforts of the hero Ram Chandra to recover his abducted wife Sita. While preparing to invade the island-fortress of Lanka, where his wife was being held captive, Ram built a bridge of floating stones; the stones did not sink because on each of them was inscribed the name "Ram," which is also an epithet for God. "To float across" is a proverbial expression for "salvation."

Each song in The Adi Granth contains a "Rest" verse, which summarizes the message of the entire song. As well, since The Adi Granth is structured on ragas and on their performance, the "Rest" verse serves as a chorus, which is repeated after every stanza.

These are all proverbial tales of God's enduring love for people, no matter how great the sin. "The prostitute" was given a parrot by a holy man who sought to save her from her life of iniquity. The only word the parrot could utter was "Ram." Hearing God's name being repeated day and night, the prostitute too took up the refrain and cleansed herself and achieved salvation.

"The misshapen" girl was King Kamsa's young handmaiden. Kamsa was Krishna's evil uncle who continually devised plots to kill him. One day she rubbed some sandalwood paste on Krishna's feet, mistaking him for Kamsa since she could not look up. Greatly moved, Krishna took her by her shoulders and lifted her up; she was made whole and acquired a beautiful body.

Ajamala was a Brahmin who fell in love with a prostitute, and he lived his whole life besotted with worldly pleasures. On his dying day, with his last breath, he called out to his youngest son, whose name was Narayana (an epithet for God) and at once he obtained salvation, having finally uttered the name of God.

Near the end of his life, Krishna, the hero of the epic *The Mahabharata*, lost all that he had—his city, his kingship, his family, his kin, and his beloved son, Pradyumna. In his sadness he would retreat to the great forest that surrounded his city of Dwarka. One day, as he lay beneath a tree, a hunter mistook him for a deer hiding in the thicket, and shot a poisoned arrow at him that pierced his heel (the only vulnerable spot on his whole body, much like Achilles). Before he died from the wound, Krishna forgave the hunter who thus was freed from the taint of this sinful act.

Vidura was a poor man who lived in a humble shack outside the magnificent city of the great king, Duryodhana. When Krishna visited this city, he chose to stay with Vidura rather than at the great king's palace. When Krishna took his leave of Vidura, he blessed the poor man with salvation.

Sudama was a very poor man, and Krishna's childhood friend. When Krishna became the king of Dwarka, Sudama's wife suggested that he go visit his old friend. He heeded her advice and set out, taking with him all that he had at the time—a small sackful of rice. Krishna was delighted to see him and accepted the rice with great gladness. In turn, he gave him great piles of gold, and had Sudama's humble cottage rebuilt into a wondrous palace.

Ugarsaina was the father of King Kamsa. When Krishna finally killed Kamsa, he gave the kingdom over to Ugarsaina, who was a good and kindly man.

Raga Asa:

2.

This entire hymn questions the efficacy of traditional Hindu worship of idols, to whom one should offer only pristine oblations, among which water, flowers, and milk are deemed the purest. But Namdeva points out that these elements of conventional worship are in themselves defiled, and therefore unfit for the idols. In brief, Namdeva is subverting the logic of Hindu worship by questioning its integrity.

The number of living things that are said to exist in water equal "four million, two hundred thousand," according to Hindu thought.

3.

Yama is the Hindu god of death who leads off the souls of the dead in a noose. Cf. Pluto who carries off souls in a similar fashion.

The "needle" is the guru's instruction and teaching; the "thread" is the disciple's purified heart. The two together sew the soul to God.

4.

The "crane" in Indian folklore is known for its duplicity, and here symbolizes the false stances and postures assumed by self-proclaimed holy men, whose real intent in meditating is to win personal gain—just as a crane that seems to be deeply meditating is actually looking for food. In this song, Namdeva is exposing the perfidy of those who claim to be holy men.

Raga Gujri:

1.

"Illusion" is Maya, which represents the false qualities of the world—its supposed permanence, durability, and eternity.

Idols are made of "stone" as are the footpaths that lead to the inner sanctum. Again, Namdeva is subverting traditional Hindu concepts of divinity and sanctity.

2.

The "trace" can refer both to one's caste and lineage, and to the concept that God's existence cannot be made visible.

Raga Sorath:

1.

"Word" refers to nada, the Yogic principle of sound, or shakti (cosmic energy). By uttering a mantra one can bring that energy into play within oneself.

The "lotus-room" is the heart wherein God resides.

The "eternal Sun" is God; the "lamp" is the individual soul. Both possess similar qualities, and therefore it is the ingrained desire in each to merge with the other.

2.

The traditional story associated with this song tells us that once Namdeva's little house was destroyed by fire. Being completely helpless, he did the only thing he could—he wandered off and meditated upon God's name. While he was gone, a carpenter came and overnight rebuilt the house better than the previous one. In the morning friends and neighbors marveled at Namdeva's new abode. When a neighbor's wife asked him whose handiwork this was, Namdeva burst into song, realizing that the carpenter was none other than God himself. On an allegorical level, we can read this song as God destroying the old and creating a new abode for the purified soul. The nub of the song is the idea that God is where love is.

Dhruva ("Fixed") was a sage in antiquity renowned for his saintliness. He was born a prince but was usurped by an evil cousin. Instead of fighting for his throne, he chose instead to renounce the world and to become an ascetic, thus attaining great fame and eminence. To honor him, the god Vishnu changed him into the Pole Star that never changes its position in the sky and that remains ever constant and fixed.

Sita ("Furrow"), was the wife of Ram Chandra, whose great beauty lured the evil Ravana to abduct her. This led to the conflict described in *The Ramayana*. Eventually, Ravana was defeated and Sita regained. Cf. the plot of Homer's *Illiad*.

Vibhishana ("Frightening"), was Ravana's virtuous brother who joined Ram Chandra and helped defeat Ravana. He was rewarded for his service by being made king of Lanka.

3.

The contradictions (ultvansi, "upside-down speech") of the first stanza stem from Yogic notions of the brain, which is said to be the vessel wherein God's essence is distilled and then personally "tasted." The "drum" is the brain that heats up when breath is diverted to it. "Thunder" is the push of *kundalini* energy that opens the Tenth Door, the highest section of the brain. When this "door" opens, the "rain" of ambrosia falls upon the tongue. This process describes the physical pleasure of directly experiencing the Divine.

The heart, like the pitcher, can only be filled by God when it is plunged and submerged in Him.

Raga Dhanashri:

1.

The ascetic Markanda, the Indian Methuselah, lived all his long life in makeshift shelters in the forest.

"Mine, mine, said the Kauravas," refers to the story line of *The Mahabharata*, which describes the internecine struggle of two sets of cousins, the Pandavas and the Kauravas, for the kingdom of Hastinapur. The struggle ended with a major battle between the two factions on the field of Kurukshetra. The villain in the story is Duryodhana, who is the eldest of a hundred brothers, all of whom are killed in the great battle. *The Mahabharata* has over ninety thousand stanzas and is the longest epic poem in the world. The written text dates from about A.D. 300–400, although earlier layers are said to date from about the earliest Aryan settlements of northern India (ca. 1700–1500 B.C.).

Durvasa ("Ill-Clad") was an evil-tempered sage who lived in Dwarka, the city whose king was Krishna. One day a few young men of the Yadava clan (Krishna's tribe) played a practical joke on the sage. One of them dressed as a girl, tied an iron pot on his belly (in order to look pregnant), and went to ask the sage if he could tell the sex of the unborn child. Durvasa saw through the ruse, lost his temper, and cursed them all saying that whatever was born from that pot would utterly destroy the Yadavas. Greatly perturbed, the youths rushed to Krishna and told him about the curse. Krishna advised them to utterly destroy the pot by filing it away. The youths neglected to file the last little piece, which they threw far out to sea. Where the iron filings fell, hard reeds shot up, and the little piece of iron was swallowed by a fish, which was caught by a fisherman who retrieved the piece of iron and made an arrowhead out of it.

One day, the Yadava youths were wandering about drunk when a quarrel broke out among them; nearby were the hard reeds growing thick and strong. Some of the youths pulled up the reeds and began to run the others through. The massacre continued until all the young men were slaughtered. In this brawl, Krishna's beloved son, Pradyumna, lost his life, as did Bala Ram, Krishna's brother.

In great sorrow, Krishna one day lay down in a thicket. The fisherman, who had caught the fish and made an arrowhead from the little piece of iron, saw Krishna's foot and mistook it for a deer hiding in the bushes. He shot his arrow and struck Krishna on the heel, his sole vulnerable spot. Krishna died from the wound after forgiving the hunter. Thus was Durvasa's curse fulfilled, and all the Yadavas perished.

2.

This entire hymn relies upon notions of Yogic physiology.

The "ten ascetics" are the organs of action (mouth, hands, feet, genitals, and excretory organs), and the organs of perception (sight, touch, taste, sensation, and sound).

The "five" are evil passions, that is, greed, pride, worldly love, anger, and lust.

The "seventy-two" are the number of blood vessels found in the heart, according to Yogic concepts.

"Pleading, I fall at His feet" hints at an episode in *The Ramayana* when Ram Chandra wins Sita as his wife by drawing Shiva's great bow. In anger, his rival, Parasa Ram, came at him with his ax, but Ram Chandra did not confront him; instead he fell at his feet and pleaded with him to let his anger go. Parasa Ram softened, and the two become fast friends.

"Why wander and roam around?" refers to the practice of renouncing the world and becoming a wandering mendicant.

3.

"Marwar" is a region in the Thar desert.

Indra, besides being the king of the gods, is also god of rain and lightning.

Chakava-birds (ruddy sheldrake) are found in pairs, it is said, because they possess the souls of pining lovers. When the sun sets, the pair must part, and all night long each calls out to the other, as they wait to unite again with the rising sun.

Mansarowar is the sacred Lake Manasa in the Himalayas, near Tibet. It is said to contain countless pearls—the only thing swans can eat, according to Indian folklore. Swans can also separate milk from water with their beaks. Hansa (Swan) is also the soul that flies away from the body after death.

The *chatrik*, or "the pied cuckoo," lives only on raindrops, as legend has it, and therefore eagerly awaits the monsoon rains.

4.

Maya is an integral part of God's creation, and thus emanates from Him. He casts His creatures into illusion through which they must find Him. This is God's play or *lila*.

God's garden consists of five qualities, three of which belong directly to him, namely, truth, conscience, and bliss; the other two belong to Maya, that is, form and identity. All creatures carry these qualities within them.

The "well-pot" refers to a Persian wheel that has pots tied to its outer rim that plunge in and out of water—just as a soul plunges in and out of the world through reincarnation.

Raga Todi:

1.

This song is another instance of ultvansi (upside-down speech) which calls into question normality in order to demonstrate the illusory nature of worldly reality.

2.

Orthodox Hindus fast on the eleventh day of each month.

3.

Much ink has been spilled on this playful song, beginning with the problematic "Rest" verse, which is only a single line. The "three things" can be construed as the three virtues, or gunas (literally, "strands"), which are light, goodness, and darkness. From these three strands matter and creation are woven.

One of the functions of Brahmins is to draw up "horoscopes" for newborn children.

The worship of the lingam (phallus) is part of the cult of Shiva.

Shyama (dusky) is an epithet for Krishna who was raised by foster-parents in the village of Gokul, inside the forest of Bindraban (Vrindavana).

Raga Tilang:

1.

This hymn is mostly in Persian with a little admixture of Old Hindi. In northern India, with the Muslim rule (ca. 1000 A.D. until the British takeover some eight hundred years later), Persian was the lingua franca.

2.

This hymn is also a mixture of Persian and Old Hindi.

Mongol is a generic term for a Muslim. Namdeva finds it odd that a Muslim is going to Dwarka, a Hindu holy city.

Khan is a common term for a Muslim nobleman. It is Turkic in origin and means "king" or "ruler" (cf. Genghis Khan). On a primary level, Namdeva is pointing out the fact that the stranger is the only Muslim among the many Hindu pilgrims. More precisely, the implication is that God is the "Khan" of the world.

The "lord of horses" is Surya the sun god. The "lord of elephants" is Indra. The "lord of men" is Brahma. All of these gods are themselves creations of God.

Raga Gaund:

1.

The horse sacrifice (ashva medha) was the most potent of sacrifices in Vedic times. The ritual is described in detail in *The Rig Veda* and has cognates in other Indo-European societies. The rite consisted of the following: a pure white horse would be consecrated and allowed to roam freely for a year; it would be followed by a band of chosen warriors. At the end of the year, it was captured and, on a designated day, slaughtered with an ax before the king. The queen then would ritually copulate with the dead horse to ensure fertility. The animal would then be cut up and its meat boiled in a large caldron. The cooked meat would then be eaten by Brahmins and royalty. For Indo-European cognates cf. the Roman *october equus* and the account given by Gerald of Wales in his *History and Topography of Ireland*, chapter 102.

Gaya is one of the holiest shrines in Hinduism, where grains are offered to the *Pitri* (forefathers). Cf. *manes* in Roman tradition.

Asi is a stream that flows near Benares (Varanasi), the city sacred to the god Shiva. It is said that those who die in Benares immediately gain salvation, such is its holiness.

The "six duties" are those that every Brahmin must perform: reciting the *Vedas*, teaching the *Vedas*, observing proper rituals, performing those rituals for others, receiving alms, and giving alms to other Brahmins.

The "dialogues" are the *Tantras*, the sacred books of Tantricism, which take the form of dialogues between Shiva and his wife Parvati.

3.

Narada was one of Brahma's sons, and Dhruva's guru. Once he approached the absolute Godhead and demanded to know the secret to Maya. In order that he may know, Vishnu appeared to him and commanded him to carry out various deeds, one of which involved becoming a woman. Cf. the story of Teiresias.

For Dhruva, see *Raga Sorath*, 2.

5.

Harnakhasa ("Golden-eyed") was a devotee of Shiva and the father of Prahlada ("Joyous"), the legendary saint in whose defense Vishnu took on the fearful incarnation of *Narsingh* ("Man-Lion"). Harnakhasa was angered at his son's lack of respect for Shiva and one day tied him to a pillar, drew out his sword, and threatened to kill him if he did not obey him. Mockingly he asked Prahlada, "Where is your god now?" In answer, Vishnu emerged from the pillar in the guise of *Narsingh*, and tore apart Harnakhasa with his claws, thus saving Prahlada his devotee.

Putana ("Stinking") was Krishna's wet-nurse whom the evil king Kamsa sent to Gokul to kill the infant Krishna who was the legitimate heir to the throne of Dwarka but whom Kamsa had usurped. Putana poisoned her nipples and gave them to Krishna to suckle. The infant not only sucked out all the milk but her life-breath as well. Before she died, she called upon God for forgiveness and thus was saved.

"Draupada's daughter" is Draupadi, the joint wife of the five Pandava brothers. She was won in a gambling match by the Kauravas and as they were ripping off her clothes, she prayed to God and was saved from rape and dishonor.

Gautama was a pious sage who dwelled by the Ganges and was married to the beautiful Ahlaya. Every day before dawn, he would go to the river to bathe and meditate. While he was away, the god Indra would secretly visit Ahlaya and make love to her. One night, Ahlaya had a great desire for Indra and contrived to get her husband out of the house by telling him that it was nearly dawn and time for his meditation. When Gautama came to the river, the Ganges spoke and said that it was still night and he had been deceived by the brightness of the full moon. Gautama turned back and found his little daughter sitting by the door. When he entered, he found Ahlaya in the arms of Indra. In great anger, he cursed the god and at once a thousand vaginas covered Indra's body; in great shame the god quickly fled. Next Gautama cursed Ahlaya and she turned to stone. Much later, as Ram Chandra was passing by the Ganges, he touched this same stone with his foot and Ahlaya again was restored to her human form.

Kesi ("Hairy") was a demon sent by King Kamsa to kill Krishna. Kesi took the shape of a horse and went to Gokul. Krishna discerned the demon in the horse and tore him apart.

Kaliya ("Black) was a giant snake in the River Jamuna that Krishna beat and trampled senseless. When the snake discovered the identity of his adversary, he bowed in adoration. He then departed the river in peace, taking with him his wives and children.

6.

Bhairava ("Frightening") is one of the eight incarnations of Shiva; he is shown riding a black dog.

Sitala ("Calming") is the goddess of smallpox; her mount is a donkey.

Shiva's mount is a white bull named Nandi ("Happy").

The "Great Mother" is shakti, the female creative energy, represented as the wife of Shiva. She is known by many names: Parvati, Durga, Kali, Chandi, Oma, Sati, Devi, and Gauri.

Bhavani ("Keeper of the World") is an epithet for Durga, the Great Mother.

The *Gita*, of course is *The Bhagavad Gita* ("Song of the Lord") which outlines the principles of the bhakti-marg ("path of devotion"). The Song itself is uttered by Krishna and addressed to Arjuna, one of the Pandavas, on the battlefield of Kurukshetra; it forms a major part of *The Mahabharata*. The *Gita*'s importance as a religious text stems from the fact that it marks a clear break from the older sacrifice- and ritual-based theology to a doctrine grounded in personal love and devotion for the Divine.

Raga Bilaval-Gaund:

7.

Gayatri ("Song") is considered the most sacred verse in *The Rig Veda*, and is recited day and night by pious Hindus. It is from the tenth *Mandala*, hymn 62, verse 10. The text runs thus:

> Let us therefore meditate
> upon the luminous radiance of Savitr
> that he may illumine our minds
> so we may shine like the gods.

The god Savitr ("Animator") is the sun. *Gayatri* is also a Vedic meter containing three lines of eight syllables each. The first four syllables are free, while the last four must be stressed as short-long-short-long/short (v—,v—/v). This meter is also known as the "limping meter" because of its short-long structure. This "limp" is explained by the following mythological account. Once, during an important sacrifice, Brahma's wife Sarasvati failed to be present despite several summons by the god. Since Brahma needed a wife in order to complete the sacrifice, he married a girl named Gayatri and fulfilled the requirements of the rite. When Sarasvati found out about the marriage, there was a great quarrel between the two wives with the result that Sarasvati cursed Gayatri to roam the earth as a cow. Gayatri liked to graze at one particular field; but when the owner of the field found her spoiling his crop, he hit her with a club and broke one of her legs. Ever thereafter, Gayatri limped. It is interesting to note that this meter is similar to the Greek and Latin iambic, especially the Choliambic, which is also called the limping meter.

Lodha is a common name for a farmer in the region around the River Jamuna.

Raga Ramkali:

1.

This hymn was supposedly addressed to Trilochan who admonished Namdeva that he was too busy with his cloth trade to fully meditate upon the Divine. However, Namdeva reminds Trilochan that persons may do all worldly chores and still keep their thoughts fixed upon God.

A house with "ten high gates" is proverbial for a great manor.

2.

The Vedas, The Puranas, and *The Shastras* are Hindu Scriptures. There are four *Vedas* (which describe rituals for appeasing the gods), eighteen

Puranas (which relate the deeds of the gods), and six *Shastras* (which are Hindu philosophical systems). They are *Nyaya Shastra* (logic and epistemology), *Vaisheshika Shastra* (physics and science), *Sankhya Shastra* (ontology), *Yoga Shastra* (physical science), *Mimansa Shastra* (exegesis and phenomenology), and *Vedanta Shastra* (metaphysics).

"Closing the breaths" refers to Yogic breath control in order to heat the brain so that it can distill ambrosia—the nearest thing to physically experiencing the Divine. Breath is drawn up through the left nostril (the ira) while saying "Om" (God) sixteen times. The breath is stopped at the bridge of the nose where the two nostrils are said to meet. The breath is then slowly exhaled through the right nostril (the pingala), while again saying "Om" sixteen times. Next, breath is forced up to the brain through the "Tenth Door," the mystical opening at the bottom of the brain, which opens upon the Divine. At this stage, the brain becomes heated and distills ambrosia that drips onto the tongue allowing the Yogi to taste the union of the mortal and the Divine taking place within him. The left nostril is also called the Moon and the right nostril the Sun.

There are "sixty-eight" important Hindu shrines and holy places in India.

Silence (sunya) is the perfect abode of the supreme Godhead, and is beyond descriptive sound or language of any kind.

3.

The devotees of Vishnu wear necklaces made from "sweet basil" wood. Namdeva tells us that the worshiper of the supreme Godhead possesses the fruits of Yoga and personal devotion (bhakti).

4.

According to Hindu practice, bathing in holy rivers washes away sin. The river Godavari ("Cow-Giver") flows from Maharashtra to the Bay of Bengal.

Kedara is located in the Himalayas, near Garhwal, and is a shrine sacred to Shiva. It is situated on a glacier at an altitude of 11,753 feet. The temple at the shrine houses an image of Shiva as a bull. He took this shape when he fled from the battle of Kurukshetra after being defeated by the Pandavas. He ran with such urgency that he did not see a mountainside and smashed right into the sheer rock, so that only his backside was visible. This is now shown as a shapeless mass of rock, greatly venerated by pilgrims. His crushed body parts were scattered in four other regions, where shrines also exist. His arms fell at Tungnath, his mouth at Rudranath, his navel at Madhyameshwar, and his head and hair at Kalapeshwar. Collectively, these shrines are known as the "Five Kedaras."

Gomti ("Cow-Feeder") is a river in Oudh, in eastern India.

Jasrath is the Hindi equivalent of the Sanskrit Dasratha ("Ten Chariots"), the father of Ram Chandra, the hero of the epic *Ramayana*. Ram Chandra is an incarnation of the god Vishnu.

Raga Maligaura:

1.

This entire song is in praise of Krishna, the incarnation of Vishnu.

Devaki was the natural mother of Krishna, but he was raised by his foster-parents Nanda and his wife Yashodha. King Kamsa, Krishna's cousin, contrived to kill him to clear his way to the throne. To save him, his father Vasudeva whisked him away to Gokul, a village deep in the forest of Bindraban (Vrindavana).

2.

Vishnu has four arms and in each hand he holds a discus (chakra or sudarshana), an iron mace (kamodki), a conch, and a lotus.

The "elephant" was a celestial musician cursed to take the form of an elephant. One day as he was bathing in a pond, a giant sea-creature seized him and began to drag him away. In desperation, the elephant plucked a lotus flower and held it high in his trunk as an offering to God, and at once he was saved, and given back his celestial shape.

Duhshasana was the brother of Duryodhana and was one of a hundred sons of King Dhrtarashtra—all of whom were killed in the great battle of Kurukshetra (see *Raga Gaund* 5 for more details).

Raga Maru:

"All salvation" refers to the four stages of salvation identified by Hindu theology. These are saloyah (dwelling with God in heaven), samipya (being near God), sarupya (taking on God's form), and sayujya (blending with, and becoming, God).

"All power" refers to the eight siddhis. These are anuma (the capacity to shrink until one becomes invisible), mahima (the ability to grow large without limitation), garuvata (the capability to gain weight ceaselessly), laghuma (the power to become weightless), prapti (the skill to pass through objects without hindrance), vasi karna (the ability to render others completely powerless), ishta (the facility to acquire endless glory), and kama (the power to fulfill all earthly desires).

There are four "ages" (yugas): krata- (or satya-) yuga, treta-yuga, dvapara-yuga, and kali-yuga. These correspond to the four Greek ages (gold, silver, copper, and iron), and represent a similar scheme of degeneration. The names of the yugas are taken from the terms for the throw of dice, namely, cater, trey, deuce, and ace.

An "umbrella" symbolizes royalty.

Ambarika was a king of Ayodhya and one of Ram Chandra's ancestors.

The "nine treasures" are the riches of Kubera, the god of wealth. These include all the precious metals and stones, gems, jewels, and minerals. The expression is proverbial for all the wealth of the world.

Bali ("Powerful") was the son of Prahlada. He acquired great spiritual power through fervent meditation and came to control the three worlds (earth, sky, and middle-air, i.e., the space in-between). Seeing Bali's limitless power, the gods asked Vishnu to intervene since the ascetic would soon become a threat to them. Accordingly, Vishnu took on his fifth incarnation of Vamana, the dwarf. He went to Bali and asked for as much land as he could cover in three steps. In amusement, Bali accepted. At once the dwarf became a giant, and with the first step covered all the earth; with the second step he covered all of heaven, and with the third step he covered all of middle-air. Bali was left only the nether regions. But because of his great power as an ascetic, Vishnu agreed to stand at his door and be at his beck and call.

Raga Bhairo:

4.

Srirang is an epithet for Vishnu, and means the "Lover of Sri" (i.e., the goddess Lakshmi, his wife). It is used in South India.

5.

Horses from Central Asia, especially Bukhara and Samarkand, were much prized.

6.

"King of the Yadavas" is Krishna, who led the Yadava clan. See *Raga Dhanashri* 1.

The "miracle" of the temple turning to face Namdeva because he was not allowed to worship inside it because of his low caste, is an important detail in all hagiographic accounts of the life of Namdeva.

8.

This hymn explicates the dangers of being entangled with Maya, or the illusion that is the world.

Parrots are said to be fond of eating the pods of the silk tree. But soon enough their beaks get entangled in the silken threads and they cannot break free, and thus perish.

9.

For the story behind this song, see *Raga Gaund* 5.

Sanda and Marka were the teachers of the child Prahlada.

"He has conquered / the whole world" refers to Harnakhasa, Prahlada's tyrannical father.

10.

This song explicates the often violent relationship that existed in northern India between the Muslim rulers and their Hindu subjects. The Muslims looked upon Hindus as idolatrous infidels, who were perpetually subject to forced conversions, while the Hindus saw the Muslims as untouchable barbarians.

Tradition states that Namdeva was hauled before the sultan Muhammad bin Tughlaq (1325–51), who tried to force him to convert to Islam. Of course, it is impossible to know if this is legend or fact. Kabir similarly suffered an identical trial before King Sikander Lodi (1488–1516), and Guru Nanak was tried by Babur (1483–1530).

"Khuda" is a Persian (hence Muslim) epithet for God.

Elephants were often used to execute criminals. The practice consisted of tying the victim upon the earth, and the elephant would be goaded to step on his head.

"*Qazis*" are Muslim judges, and "*Mullahs*" are Islamic clerics.

Garuda ("Devourer") is the king of birds, in Hindu mythology, and the mount of Vishnu. He has the head, beak, wings, and talons of an eagle; and the body of a man.

"I am your cow" is idiomatic for a helpless person in need of care and protection.

11.

The "highest stage" (param-pada) is union with God. In yogic terms it is when the kundalini unites with Shiva in the sahasrara (also known as the

"Lotus"), which is the sphere of energy found at the very top of the sushumna vein, where the Tenth Door is located, beyond which resides the Divine. The sushumna is the spinal cord along which are found the six chakras, or "spheres of energy."

"You shall return the bed" refers to the previous hymn (*Bhairo* 10). When the sultan had been vanquished in his efforts to convert Namdeva to Islam, he gave him a golden bed as a peace offering, which Namdeva promptly threw into the Ganges. When the sultan heard of this, he asked Namdeva to return the gift. The saint called out to the river and immediately six similar beds appeared on the bank. These Namdeva sent to the sultan.

The "discus" is an emblem of Vishnu; his devotees paint it on their bodies as a sign of devotion.

The "twelve *lingams*" refers to the twelve *lingam* shrines sacred to Shiva. The better known of these are Somnath, Badri Narayana, Kedara, Visheshwar, Rameshwar, Nageshwar, Baijnath, and Bhimshankar. Lingam literally means "phallus" and constitutes phallic worship within Hinduism.

The *Puranas* ("Old") are the eighteen Hindu holy books that recount the deeds of the gods.

12.

In this song, Namdeva is deliberately mixing Hindu and Muslim terminologies in order to stress the fact that God is nonsectarian. In Hindu society, Namdeva is rejected because of his low caste, hence the reference that his cymbals were snatched away as he sang in a temple. And in Muslim society he is an infidel because he is a low-caste Hindu. Thus in both societies, Namdeva has no place—hence his theology of a God free from sectarian propriety.

A "*Qalandar*" is a long-haired Muslim holy man who has abandoned the world and all earthly possessions, very much like a Yogi. The appellation "*Qalandar* Keshava," for Keshava is also a deliberate mixture of Muslim and Hindu terminology.

Abdalis are a sect of Muslim fakirs, who wear a pointed hat, a long robe, and carry a staff.

"Fifty-six million clouds" is the number said to exist according to Indian cosmography.

Muslim cosmology states that there are eight worlds above and below the earth; other sources say that there are fourteen such worlds.

Kamla ("Lotus") is another name for Lakshmi, the wife of Vishnu.

Raga Basant:

1.

Ganges and Godavari are sacred rivers where Hindus bathe to wash away their sins.

3.

The "cart" is the body, filled with worldly sin (the "dirty laundry"). The "launderer" is the guru, and his wife is the Word (shabad). It is the Word that leads the soul to the guru, who then cleanses it in the "water tank" of divine grace.

Raga Sarang:

1.

The "benumbing fruit" is the datura, or the thorn apple, which can render a person unconscious. It was used by the thags (members of the cult of Thuggee), who ritually strangled people as a sacrifice to the goddess Kali. The unsuspecting victim was given a drink laced with datura, and then he was strangled.

3.

This entire hymn is spoken by God to Namdeva.

The "three pains" are adhi (mental pain), viadhi (physical pain), and upadhi (inflicted pain).

Raga Malar:

1.

The "seven regions" refers to the division of the earth according to Hindu geography.

Lakshmi ("Lucky") is the wife of Brahma, and the goddess of wealth and beauty.

Ishvar ("Lord") is Shiva as god of the Yogis.

Chitra and Gupta ("Visible" and "Hidden") are the recording scribes of Yama, the god of death, who write down all the deeds, good and bad, committed by a person.

Dharamraja ("King of Justice") is another name for Yama, the god of death.

"Shiva's hosts" are the ganas, a band of warriors commanded by Ganesha whose very name means the "Lord of Hosts."

Kurma ("Tortoise") is Vishnu's second incarnation. A demon named Rahu ("Seizing") once stole the ambrosia (amrita) which keeps the gods immortal and powerful and hence is their food. (Cf. ambrosia in Greek myth.) Rahu took the ambrosia and hid it deep in the World Ocean. The gods began to lose their vigor. Vishnu then suggested that the gods, with the help of the giants, churn the World Ocean. They used Mount Mandara, their dwelling place, as a churn-stick, around which they circled the World Snake Vasuki. The gods held one end, the giants the other; together they rotated Mandara as a churn.

This churning brought forth the goddess Lakshmi, Uccaihrashvas ("High-eared") the white horse of the sun god, Airavata the white elephant that Indra took as his mount, and the fabulous gem Kaustubha that Vishnu placed upon his chest. Further churning turned the water into poison and from it emerged Jyeshtha ("Eldest"), the goddess of misfortune. After more churning emerged Dhanvantri, the physician of the gods; in his hand he held a pure white cup that contained the purloined ambrosia.

All the gods rushed to drink the elixir. But the first to take it was Rahu the demon who took a quick sip. Before he could swallow, Vishnu beheaded him with his discus; his body perished; his head became immortal because of the ambrosia. His head still survives and chases the sun and moon that he swallows from time to time (hence lunar and solar eclipses). Since he has no body, the sun and the moon eventually emerge. Cf. Norse myth where the sun and the moon are chased by two bodiless wolves, Skoll and Hati.

The Ganges is here referred to as Sursari, or the "Stream of the Gods."

Arjuna ("Silvery Pale"; cf. Latin *argentum*) was one of the five Pandavas who fought the Kauravas at Kurukeshetra. Krishna was his charioteer, and it was to him that he revealed his divinity and recited *The Bhagavad Gita*.

Amrika ("Sky-Like") was a king of Ayodhya and an ancestor of Ram Chandra.

Narada ("Giving to Man") one of Brahma's sons who was a most wise sage. In order to learn the secret of Maya, he was changed, Teiresias-like, into a woman and back again into a man.

Nejaya ("Invincible") was an ancient sage about whom little is known. He was the son of Dharma by Kriya.

The Siddhas ("Accomplished") are semidivine beings who reside in middle-air. They have great miraculous powers.

The "fifty-two heroes" were a select group of warriors in Vedic society chosen to serve the gods.

2.

Shudras are the lowest of the four Hindu castes, which in descending order are Brahmins, warriors, artisans, and Shudras (who do menial tasks).

NOTES TO THE SONGS OF RAVI DASS

Raga Gauri-Guareri:

2.

This song stresses the fact that in the ideal, heavenly city, caste plays no importance whatsoever. A low-caste person is deemed a friend of all the citizens—an impossible concept in traditional Hindu society.

Raga Gauri-Bairagan:

The "safflower" was used to give a quick, delible pale yellow dye to cloth. The madder dye comes from the root of the madder vine (*rubia cordifolia*) and yields a reddish dye that is very fast. It was once widely cultivated in India, as well as in Holland and France.

Raga Gauri-Purbi:

The story of the "frogs" in the "well" is used to describe ignorance. Once there was a flood, and a frog that used to live in the rivers of the plains got washed into a well. When the water subsided, this frog was stranded and had to live out his days in the well, with all the other frogs. Often he would tell these frogs of the great bodies of water that could be found in the world. But the well-frogs laughed and ridiculed him, calling him mad, because everyone knew that the water in the well was all there was in the whole world.

Raga Gauri-Bairagan:

Proverbially, elephants are considered to be extremely patient by nature. "Achieving purity" is a work of great patience.

Raga Asa:

1.

It is said that the "deer" yearns to hear the hunter's horn (hence the ears are its vice), the "fish" is driven by taste (for that reason the tongue is its vice), the "bumblebee" longs for the perfume of the flower (therefore the nose is its vice), the "moth" desires the flame (so the eyes are its vice), and the "elephant" is driven by lust (consequently, the genitals are its vice).

However, human beings are impelled and driven by all five of these vices.

2.

The "gem" is the magical Chintaman that grants all wishes and desires.

Raga Gujri:

Like Namdeva's hymn (*Gauri* 2), Ravi Dass questions the supposed purity of traditional elements of sacrifice and worship. All things have ultimately been "used" and touched and hence are unclean and impure.

"Snakes" are said to be attracted to the perfume of sandalwood and coil themselves around sandal-trees.

Raga Sorath:

1.

The story goes that in the dark a "rope" can be mistaken for a "serpent," causing much uproar in the house.

2.

The "fish" after being eaten makes the eater thirsty.

The "few" are Brahmins who alone can be dispensers of religious learning in Hinduism.

The "pain" is the soul's separation from its Beloved, that is, God.

4.

There are "five heavenly trees." They are Mandara, Parijatika, Santana, Kalapvaruksha, and Harichandanma.

The "cow" is Kamdhenu (churned from the World Ocean by the gods), which brings about all wishes and desires.

The "four goals" are the chief aims of human existence, namely, dharma (observing religious duty), artha (acquiring wealth), kama (achieving all earthly desires), and moksha (obtaining salvation).

The "eighteen powers" are the abilities to subject all of the three worlds to one's control.

Vyasa ("Compiler") is the compiler of the four *Vedas* and the author of *The Mahabharata*.

5.

In Indian folklore, mountains are said to be the usual habitats of peacocks.

It is commonly believed that the partridge (chakor) bursts into song when it sees the full moon, for which it yearns the whole month long.

6.

"Three yards and a half" is the measurement of a pyre.

7.

This song expounds the importance of not being tied to the ways of the world. Things such as "knots," "awls," "knives," and "stitches" represent longings and desires, necessities that continually keep one preoccupied with the world.

Raga Dhanashri:

3.

Arati is the concluding ceremony at night in Hindu worship. A tray, holding lit lamps, sandalwood, saffron, flowers and various offerings, is waved before an idol as a blessing. The various items mentioned in this song are traditional elements for *arati*. In Sikh worship, *arati* refers to the concluding ceremony when final prayers are read and The Adi Granth is put away for the night.

The "grate" is used to scrape sandalwood in order to release its scent.

Raga Jaitsari:

The "five" are the evil passions: pride, lust, wrath, avarice, and worldly love.

Gautama's wife was Ahlaya who was loved by the god Indra, who was cursed by Gautama and his body sprouted a thousand vaginas. See Namdeva's song *Gaund 5* for details of this myth.

Oma is Parvati, the Great Mother and the wife of Shiva.

The "head-holder" is Shiva. This epithet refers to the myth of Brahma's lust for one of his own daughters. She tried to escape his amorous pursuits but each time he found her out. Finally in order to control Brahma's lust, Shiva cut off one of his heads (Brahma has four heads). This put a stop to his lust, but the severed head stuck to Shiva's hand because he had sinned in spilling the blood of a god. In order to have the head removed, Shiva had to visit various shrines and holy places.

Raga Suhi:

1.

"Sirat" is the bridge that spans the burning fire of Hell, according to Muslim belief. It is said to be as narrow as a single strand of hair and as sharp as a sword. All souls must walk across it. The sinful shall fall into Hell, while the righteous shall walk across to Paradise.

3.

According to Hindu custom, a body must be cremated within twenty-four hours of death.

After death, the soul of the departed is perceived as a pret ("ghoul" or "phantom") which cannot go to heaven or take on a new body, but that hovers around its relatives, and can bring them harm. To speed it on its way, it is offered water, milk, and food for ten days, after which time it becomes a spirit and goes on its way.

Raga Bilaval:

2.

"Doms" are low-caste minstrels and cremation-ground attendants (who actually burn the corpse). From this caste the Gypsies of Europe originate.

Chandals are casteless untouchables whose primary function is to carry corpses to the cremation ground. Literally, the term means, "Dog-eater" or "Cruel."

Raga Gaund:

1.

"Mukand" literally means "Savior."

2.

For *lingam*- or phallic-worship, see Namdeva *Bhairo* 11.

Providing "public wells" and "ponds" for drinking water for animals are considered meritorious acts.

During eclipses, Hindus bathe in the pools of holy shrines to ward off any evil consequences of solar or lunar eclipses. Kurukshetra is one such shrine where the faithful bathe.

"Offering" one's wife, all adorned in gold and jewels, to a Brahmin is an ancient custom and is deemed a pious act. The offering tends to be symbolic. An offering to Brahmins of any sort is considered a great deed with rewards in the hereafter.

Raga Maru:

1.

The "touch" (and even the shadow) of a low-caste person can defile a member of the upper castes.

2.

With a few exceptions, this song is the same as *Sorath* 4. See the notes for explanations.

Raga Kedara:

For the "six duties" that Brahmins must perform, see Namdeva, *Gaund* 1.

Valmiki was a *chandal* hunter, much devoted to Krishna, who was not given food during the celebrations marking the end of the battle between the Kauravas and the Pandavas. When Krishna learned that Valmiki had been turned away because of his caste, he ordered that Draupadi herself, the royal wife of the Pandavas, go to Valmiki and feed him. Then Krishna himself washed the hunter's feet. This act was to demonstrate that a low-caste man who loves God is superior to a negligent Brahmin.

The *chandal* Valmiki should not be confused with Valmiki the Brahmin, the author of *The Ramayana*.

For "Ajamala," the "courtesan," the "hunter," and the "elephant," see Namdeva, *Gauri Cheti*. For the elephant, see Namdeva, *Maligauri* 2.

Raga Basant:

Ravens as despoilers of dead bodies are a traditional literary motif. Cf. Norse and Anglo-Saxon heroic literature where ravens serve a similar function.

Raga Malar:

1.

The "city" is Benares, present-day Varanasi.

2.

Kamlapati ("Lord of Kamla or Lakshmi") is Vishnu.

The "calico-printer" is Namdeva.

Sanaka ("Ancient") was the first of Brahma's four mind-born sons. The other three were Sanandana, Sanatana, and Sanata Kumara. All four were renowned for their great purity and ascetic powers.

The "seven islands" are the seven continents.

Muslims observe two "religious festivals" or eids, namely, eid-ul-addha (eid of sacrifice) and eid-ul-fitr (eid of fast breaking). During eid-ul-addha cows and sheep are sacrificed in remembrance of Abraham's sacrifice of his son. Eid-ul-fitr comes at the end of the month of Ramadan.

"Sheikhs" and *"pirs"* are Muslim spiritual leaders and guides.

3.

The "dirty clothes" are the sins of a lifetime.

The "shop" is the body that ever deals in falsehood.

NOTES TO THE SONGS OF JAYADEVA

Raga Maru:

The first section of this song describes Yogic breath control that allows the practitioner to ultimately "taste" or to physically experience the Divine. For a more in-depth description see the note to Namdeva, *Raga Ramkali* 2.

"Victorious Deva" is a pun on Jayadeva's own name, which means God (or Deva's) victory (*Jaya*).

NOTES TO THE SONGS OF TRILOCHAN

Sri Raga:

"Friends" refers to human gurus.

"Forests and glades" is an idiomatic expression for "all over, everywhere."

Raga Gujri:

1.

According to tradition, this song is addressed to four individuals, each of whom represents a particular Hindu sect.

The first two lines are spoken to an udasi (mendicant). The next two lines are addressed to a sanyasi (wandering ascetic).

The Rest stanza is uttered to one Jaya Chandra, a Brahmin.

The next two stanzas are addressed to a Nath Yogi. And the two lines before the signature couplet are to a kapri, a sect of wandering holy men who cover their bodies with long cloaks and carry wooden bowls out of which they drink water.

Raga Dhanashri:

Tradition says that this song was addressed by Trilochan to his wife, who complained that the life of holiness was too difficult and poverty-ridden. To console her, Trilochan pointed out that their poverty was the result not of their dedication to God, but because of their past misdeeds.

In this song, Trilochan is apposing association with the sacred with the weight of past deeds. In each example, he shows that despite proximity to holiness, the laws of Karma still had to be fulfilled, wherein deeds and misdeeds are rewarded or punished.

The crescent moon adorns the brow of Shiva.

Each night the moon submerges into the sacred river Ganges, where it rests all day and again rises at night.

The moon is also the progenitor of the Lunar Dynasty of kings, chief among whom was Krishna, here called Sarangdhar (Holder of the bow).

The moon's "sin" consisted in this: once he fell in love with the wife of Brhaspati ("Lord of Sacred Speech") who was the priest of the gods. Unable to win her love, he abducted Brhaspati's wife and carried her off. For this sinful act, the moon's face was scarred and pocked, marks that are still visible today. (Brhaspati was later identified with the planet Jupiter.)

Aruna ("Red") was the son of Kashyapa and Vinata and was hatched prematurely from an egg by his mother. He was the charioteer of the sun god and the older brother of Garuda. His misdeed was that he cursed his mother for his lameness. Because of this action, his handicap could never be healed.

The great sage Agastya ("Moutain-Thrower") once invited the World Ocean to a feast. The Ocean refused, thus angering the sage, who scooped up all the water, drank it, and then urinated it all out. This is the reason why the oceans and seas are salty.

Hanumana ("Large-Jaws"), the monkey god, helped Ram Chandra in his fight against Ravana. When Lakshman, Ram Chandra's brother, was wounded and near death, it was Hanumana who found the magical, healing herb that cured all affliction, and brought it to Ram Chandra, much to the hero's delight. But once Hanumana robbed a holy man, taking everything except a loincloth. The holy man cursed Hanumana saying that he too would one day possess only a loincloth; never would he possess anything greater. And such was the case. Despite conquering Lanka with Ram Chandra, he got no reward.

NOTES TO THE SONGS OF BENI

Sri Raga:

"To be sung like *Paharia*" is a direction for singing this song. *Paharia* refers to a hymn by Guru Nanak, also in *Sri Raga*, which describes forms of worship for the eight watches of day and night. This association suggests that at the time of the compilation of The Adi Granth, there already existed a tradition that connected this song by Beni with Guru Nanak's song in the same measure. This further implies that Guru Nanak possessed Beni's songs.

Raga Ramkali:

This entire hymn describes the Yogic conception of physically experiencing the divine through the Tenth Door, the mystical opening in the brain. Yogic physiognomy holds that the nine natural openings of the body allow us to experience the physical world, while the Divine can only be known and experienced through the brain. The entire process depends upon breath control, wherein breath is stopped from exiting the body, and is forced to seek the only opening available to it, namely the Tenth Door. As the breath rises toward the Tenth Door, it becomes heated, and when it finally exits through the mystical opening, the brain distills ambrosia, which falls upon the tongue. This taste of ambrosia is recognized as the physical savoring of the Divine.

The *ira*-vein houses the breath of the left nostril, according to Yogic belief.

The *pingala*-vein contains the breath of the right nostril.

The *sukhmana*-vein holds the breath that gathers at the bridge of the nose.

The "one spot" is the brain.

"Holy Prayag" is a sacred spot for Hindus, where three holy rivers meet: the Ganges, the Jamuna, and the Sarasvati (which is said to flow underground). Prayag is modern-day Allahabad. The confluence of rivers is believed to be a place of great sanctity. The Yogis use Prayag as a metaphor for the convergence of the three breaths in the brain.

The "inner sky" is the brain.

The "alcove" is the cavity that is said to exist above the brain and below the Tenth Door.

The "three qualities" are sattva (light and goodness), rajas (impulse and action), and tamas (darkness and ignorance). It is said that these three qualities permeate all matter in varying degrees.

The "three worlds" are earth, middle-air, and heaven.

The "seed-mantra" is the Word (shabad) that directs the individual to the in-dwelling Divine.

The limbs of the body are often called "branches" and trees; the implication being that the mortal frame is perishable, therefore one should not lose it carelessly as in a gambling match.

The "west" is traditionally associated with ignorance, death, and evil.

"What cannot be restrained" is the breath that has been stopped from exiting the body.

The "lamp with four wicks" is divine wisdom.

In Yogic jargon, the brain is called the "lotus," whose petals are precious gems and jewels. In the center of this lotus is the Tenth Door, beyond which lives God.

The "fan" signifies kingship. The "conch" connotes divinity. In Hindu temples, the gods are awakened in the morning by the blowing of the conch-shell.

The "five types of instruments" are wind, percussion, string, metallic (e.g., cymbals and bells), and the human voice. "Five instruments" also refers to the five types of breath designated by the Yogis, that is, breath is pushed up the spinal column (the kundalini); as it is forced toward the brain, it touches five centers or chakras.

"Demons" are all evil things.

Raga Parbhati:

"Basil leaves" worn on the forehead signify renunciation of the world.

"Bathing" and changing clothes are Brahmanic rituals.

To take a vow to drink "only milk" is deemed pious among Brahmins. Milk is thought to be the purest of liquids, and therefore it is associated with Brahmins who are considered to be the purest of humans. It is also said that milk flows in the veins of Brahmins, while blood (an impure liquid) flows in the veins of others.

"Circles" drawn on the body in honor of Ganesha are four in number.

Dancing in front of an idol is a form of worship.

The "fawnskin" (mrigchhala) is used as a mat solely by great and accomplished holy men.

Vaishnavites carry rosaries of sweet "basil-wood."

The *rudrakhan* (rosary made from the red berries of the Indian beech, or hornbeam tree) is carried by Shaivites.

NOTES TO THE SONG OF RAMANANDA

Raga Basant:

This song is written from the point of view of a woman. In Indian mysticism, the individual is presented as female, while the Divine is the male beloved.

The "home" refers to the concept that one does not need to wander about like an ascetic in order to find God, for the Divine is as near as one's home or heart.

"Perfumes" and "sandal shavings" are traditional elements in Hindu worship.

"Water and stone" are the idols and sacred pools that are present in every Hindu temple.

"If I do not find Him here" refers to the heart.

NOTES TO THE SONGS OF DHANNA

Raga Asa:

2.

This is considered to be the composition of Guru Arjan Dev (the fifth Sikh Guru); its purpose is to explain the last verse of the previous song: how it was that Dhanna found God. Tradition maintains that Dhanna was given a saligram (a stone representing Vishnu) by a Brahmin. Daily Dhanna performed acts of devotion before this idol. In order to dispel this hint of idol-worship, Guru Arjan wrote this song, and here the Guru explains that Dhanna found God, not by worshiping a stone, but by following the example of worthy saints, who were all devoted to the unmanifested (nirgun) God.

3.

The "ten doors" are the actual and mystical openings in the body: the anus, the genitals, the mouth, two nostrils, two eyes, two ears, and the Tenth Door; the latter is where the Divine resides.

The fetus is said to hang upside down in the womb in a posture of penance, according to Hindu physiology. A perpetual fire is said to burn in the womb, and it comes to encircle the fetus; however, the water enclosing the unborn child protects it from the fire. The image of the womb is very much that of an oven.

Insects were commonly thought to hatch from stones, according to Hindu zoology.

Raga Dhanashri:

This is a curious genre of poetry that is frequently found in the works of the saints. Cf., for example, Kabir's song in *Raga Sorath* 11, in *Songs of Kabir from the Adi Granth* (1991), pp. 161–62. No doubt, this type of verse portrays the Divine as intimately personal in that He devises and orders even the most mundane of human needs.

"Grain grown / on a well-plowed field" refers to grain grown on a field that is plowed seven times. As well, the meaning could be "a mixture of seven types of grain." Such a mixture is often given to holy men as an offering.

NOTES TO THE SONG OF SADHNA

Raga Bilawal:

Once a carpenter's son fell in love with a princess who had sworn that she would marry only the god Vishnu himself. Desperate with love, the carpenter's son had himself fitted with two additional arms, donned the guise of the god and went to woo the princess. Soon, the two were married. Not long afterward, a rival king attacked the kingdom. However, the princess assured the people that she had Vishnu as her husband, who would save them all. She went inside and asked her husband to intervene and defeat the enemy. At his wit's end, the carpenter's son finally called out to Vishnu to save him and his honor and also to forgive him for pretending to be the god. Vishnu took pity on the carpenter's son, defeated the invaders, and gave the young man great honor.

NOTES TO THE SONGS OF SHEIKH FARID

Raga Asa:

2.

Katak is the month of October, and it the time when Demoiselle cranes migrate into India for the winter from their Eurasian breeding grounds.

March is a very dry month in the Panjab, and forest fires are common.

Savan (July/August) is the month of monsoon rains.

"That which takes / six months to form" is the human body. According to Indian belief, the fetus develops human form in the first six months of its life.

Raga Suhi:

The "deep well" is the world.

"Sharper than a sword" refers to the bridge Sirat, in Muslim belief, which spans Hell-fire, and is said to be narrow and thin as a hair and sharper than a sword. Across it, all souls must walk. The righteous shall cross over into paradise, while sinners shall fall into the fires of Hell.

Raga Suhi-Lalit:

In olden times, in the Panjab, the "safflower" was used to give a temporary dye to clothes; it yielded a bright orange or red color (depending on the cloth). It faded after one wash.

The "swan" is the soul.

NOTES TO THE SLOKAS OF SHEIKH FARID

1.

The "lord" is the angel of death, Azrael in Islamic belief.

2.

This refers to the "little bundle" of accumulated sins.

3.

"Sain" (another form of the title "Swami") refers to a human guru.

4.

Filling a hand with "sesame seeds" is part of a traditional Panjabi marriage ceremony, where the bridegroom takes a handful of sesame seeds and places them in the hands of his bride. Likewise, the bride fills her hand with seeds and gives them to the groom.

Sesame seeds can also refer to one's alloted breaths in a lifetime.

"I would have been less vain." God does not care for pride, just as in child marriages the bridegroom is not concerned how his bride looks.

5.

The "skirt" is the individual soul. The "garment" is God. The act of tying a "knot" ensures that the two do not separate.

The "hem" or "skirt" of a coat or mantle is given much importance in Panjabi verse; it was common practice to tie important things to the hem of one's garment.

6.

"Black words" are those that are destructive, negative, and hateful.

10.

"Sugar has become poison" refers to the world's sweetness that kills the soul.

11.

The "branch" is the body, which matures into the "color" of death.

13.

This sloka is by the third Sikh Guru, Amar Dass, and is meant to explain Farid's *Sloka* 12, in which Farid implies that God's love is gained through personal merit. Guru Amar Dass corrects this notion by stating that God's love cannot be gained through personal goodness; rather it is acquired through God's grace.

16.

"Grass" is symbolic of eternal patience.

22.

Here the injunction is to honor guests and friends.

23.

Bijaur is the region beyond the Swat Valley and Malakand in the present-day Northwest Frontier Provinces of Pakistan, close to the Afghan border.

29.

One should be happy with what one has and not be envious.

31.

The "wife" is the soul, the "in-laws" life after death, "parents" refers to the world, and the "husband" is God. Here Guru Amar Dass elaborates on the concept of Farid in *Sloka* 30 that a wife forsaken by her husband cannot be truly happy.

32.

Here Guru Nanak completes the exposition by stating that the wife who loves her husband ultimately belongs to him—just as the soul that loves God belongs to Him.

35.

This refers to the "separation" of a woman from her lover, of a soul from God.

37.

"Poisonous stalks" are worldly pleasures.

40.

The "gong" is not struck at night, and therefore it gets a chance to nurse its pain. Likewise, the body nurses the pain of separation from God every night.

43.

"Caesar" is synonymous with "ruler" or "king" in Persian and Panjabi.

45.

"Orphans" are traditionally deemed the most wretched in the world. Thus before death, all are equal.

48.

The "two lamps" are the eyes.

49.

"Cotton" is stretched, scoured, and beaten. "Sesame seed" is crushed for oil. "Sugarcane" is pressed for juice. "Paper" is mashed into pulp. A "clay-pot" is baked in a furnace. Coal is set on fire and burned.

50.

The "patched coat" is the suf, a sleeveless, woolen jacket worn by Muslim holy men, from which some believe the Sufis derive their name; others construe the term *sufi* as being derived from the Greek sophia (wisdom).

51.

The "body steeped in God" becomes immortal and therefore cannot bleed.

52.

Guru Amar Dass interjects at this point in order to negate any doctrinal misunderstanding caused by Baba Farid's previous sloka about a bloodless body, which can be deemed to be a reification of the Brahmanic assumption that only milk flows in the veins of Brahmins because of their inherent purity.

53.

The "lake" is the company of saints. "Pure things" are divine wisdom and enlightenment. The "pond" is this world.

54.

The "woman" is the soul.

56.

The "rooftop" is this world: one can only live a certain number of years.

58.

"That place" is the grave.

61.

Muslim holy men usually dress in "black" or white.

63.

The "virgin" is the soul within a body. Marriage is the separation of the soul from the body. The soul that did not work out its salvation while in the body regrets its marriage.

64.

"Swans" are holy men. The "brackish pond" is the world from which "swans" do not drink.

65.

"Coarse grain" is kodhra, a type of low-grade wheat; hence the world.

66.

The "birds" are souls. The "overflowing pond" is the world. The "withered lotuses" are corpses.

68.

The rope lowers the pot into the well. Here, the "pot" is the body, the "rope" life.

69.

Those "who burdened the earth" are sinners who, when they die unrepentant, cannot ever return to wipe clean their sins.

70.

Muslims are enjoined to pray "five times" a day.

75.

Guru Arjan clarifies Farid's use of the term *Hell*, since Sikh doctrine recognizes good and evil as worldly illusions. Only God is real, and He is beyond such categories.

79.

The "bird" is the soul. The image is that of guests at a caravansarai (often situated in gardens) who leave at the break of day.

80.

The "fragrant musk" is divine devotion that saints share with each other.

81.

This is the "fire" of suffering and pain.

82.

This sloka by Guru Arjan Dev clarifies the previous sloka by Farid in that everyone is not burned by the same fire, because salvation is open to all.

83.

This sloka by Guru Arjan Dev further develops the idea that the world and the body are not to be condemned as inherently evil; rather their beauty is to be used to find God.

85.

The "ferryman" is the guru who warns the individual of impending doom.

88.

The demands of desire are endless, just as the demands of people are ceaseless. If the ears are stopped up, then one can ignore the clamor, and the wind can carry it wherever it wants.

89.

"Dates" and "honey" are heavenly delights promised to each Muslim. However, Farid is saying that both of these delightful things also remind one of what lies ahead—death.

94.

Salvation is the result of personal endeavor and concern.

96.

The "little tree" is a human life, which one day shall be washed away by the river (Death). The "unfired clay jug" is the body that cannot contain the soul for too long.

97.

Muslims believe that the soul exists with the body, in the grave, until Judgment Day.

99.

The "hawk of God" is "Death." The "crane" is the soul.

100.

When Death comes, the combined strength of four brothers cannot win over it.

The "man" walking on the "shoulders of four men" is a corpse carried on a bier.

104.

Guru Amar Dass clarifies the previous sloka by Farid, in that one does not need to wear a certain type of religious garb or follow certain rituals in order to meet the divine Beloved.

105.

Guru Arjan Dev extrapolates and clarifies a further point from Farid's *Sloka* 103, in that dress, garb, and appearance can be sources of pride—even garb that is outwardly pious-seeming. Guru Arjan's point is that outer show of piety, without true love, is empty and vain.

This refers to a "hilltop after rain," that is, rain does not stay on a hill, but runs down the slope, thus leaving the top itself unquenched.

108.

Guru Arjan is elucidating Farid's *Sloka* 107 in that if loves exists between God and man, then there is no forgetting by either.

109.

Guru Arjan continues his examination of Farid's *Sloka* 107 by stating here that suffering and happiness all emanate from God and are to be accepted as such.

110.

The "world" is played like an instrument by Maya. An individual who is part of the world is also an instrument of Maya.

111.

In the last explanation of Farid's *Sloka* 107, Guru Arjan states that in order to remember God, one must be like a fakir, whose full-time occupation is none other than God.

112.

The "blossom" is devotion; the "fruit" is spiritual awakening.

113.

Guru Nanak corrects Farid's previous *sloka* by stating that rewards are God's gift of grace; they cannot be obtained by personal merit.

114.

External "searching" is useless, since the "Lord" is within.

117.

This sloka reveals the secret that Farid mentioned in *Sloka* 116: patience brings a soul closer to God.

120.

Guru Nanak again corrects Farid's previous sloka (119) in that one does not need to perform severe physical austerities in order to know the Divine.

121.

This is a further elaboration of Guru Nanak's sloka by Guru Amar Dass in that, instead of austerities, one must be pious in order to know God.

122.

The "cranes" are pretenders at piety who seek to represent themselves as "swans," or true pious men.

123.

The "crane" is a hypocrite holy man who leads trusting people astray. Cranes in the Panjab are proverbially cunning; swans are deemed patient.

124.

Guru Nanak interpolates Farid's previous sloka that holiness is a state of grace rather than an attribute acquired by personal effort.

125.

The "bird" is the soul. The "lake" with tossing waves is the world. The "poachers" are the various sins that ensnare and destroy the soul.

GLOSSARY

ADI GRANTH: ("The Primal Book") Scripture of the Sikhs, and revered as a living guru.

ADINATH: ("Primal Lord") an epithet of Shiva as Lord of Yoga.

AGASTYA: ("Mountain-Thrower") a great seer and sage who drank the World Ocean and then urinated all the water out, thus making seawater salty.

AHLAYA: ("Hard to Plow," "Virgin") wife of the sage Gautama and lover of the god Indra. For her adultery, she was cursed by Gautama and turned to stone.

AIRAVATA: ("Milk-Born") the snow-white elephant that Indra rides. It was "churned" from the World Ocean.

AJAMALA: ("Eternal Strength") a Brahmin from Kanauj who fell in love with a prostitute and by whom he had several children. In his old age, when he was about to die, the heralds of Yama came to him to take away his soul. In fear, he cried out to his youngest son named Narayana (an epithet of Vishnu). But instead of the son, Vishnu himself appeared and drove off the messengers of Yama.

ALLAH: ("Lord") Arabic for God; hence a Muslim appellation.

AMBARIKA: ("Sky-Like") a king of Ayodhya and an ancestor of Ram Chandra, the hero of the epic poem *The Ramayana*.

anahata: ("unheard") the eternal, soundless quality of sound that is present in every form of vibration, intonation and note. It is the abode of the absolute God.

arati: ("turning") the concluding ceremony in Hindu worship when a tray with lit lamps, incense, flowers and offerings is waved before an idol for blessing.

ARJAN DEV: (1563–1606) the fifth Sikh guru and compiler of The Adi Granth; he was tortured to death at Lahore fort by order of Jahangir, the Mughal emperor of India.

ARJUNA: ("Silver") the hero of the epic poem *The Mahabharata* to whom Krishna revealed his divinity by reciting *The Bhagavad Gita*. Arjuna was one of the five Pandava brothers.

ARUNA: ("Red") the charioteer of the sun god and the older brother of Garuda.

ashva-medha: ("horse-sacrifice") an ancient fertility ritual of the Aryans involving the sacrifice of a white horse. It has several parallels in other Indo-European societies.

ASI: ("Broad-Sword") a little river near Benares (Varanasi), the city holy to Shiva.

AYODHYA: ("Invincible") the capital city of the kingdom of Koshala, and the birthplace of Ram Chandra, the hero of the epic *The Ramayana*.

AZRAEL: ("The Lord's Helper") the angel of death, who separates the soul from the body, according to Muslim belief.

BAIKUNTH: ("The Immanent") the heaven in which Vishnu dwells. Also, VAIKUNTHA.

BALI: ("Offering") a demon who took control of the universe. Vishnu won it back by assuming his incarnation as a dwarf.

BANVARI: ("Wearing a Garland of Wild Flowers") an epithet for Krishna.

BHAGAVAD GITA: ("The Song of the Lord") the sermon by Krishna, addressed to Arjuna, which describes the merits of love and devotion.

BHAGVAN: ("Treasure-Giver") an epithet for Krishna.

BHAIRAVA: ("Frightening") an epithet for Shiva as lord of the chaotic dance that destroys the universe.

bhakti: ("devotion") the Hindu reform movement that stressed personal love for, and devotion to, God, and descried ritualistic religion.

BHAVANI: ("Keeper of the World") an epithet for the Great Mother.

BINDRABAN: ("Thicket of Sweet Basil") the forest surrounding the village Gokul, where Krishna grew up, and where he frolicked with the milkmaids. Also, VRINDAVANA.

BITHAL: ("The Distant") an epithet for Krishna as he is worshipped in the South of India.

BRAHMA: ("Creator") the first of the Hindu gods who created the universe.

BRAHMIN: ("Brahma-Like") the highest of the Hindu castes whose members, as priests, propagate Vedic wisdom and ritual. Cf. the Latin *Flamen*.

BUDDHA: ("Enlightened") the title of Siddhartha Gautama, the founder of Buddhism; also considered one of Vishnu's incarnations.

chakava: ("watcher") the ruddy sheldrake or the brahmani duck. It is used as an emblem for love in poetry. It is said that ducks live in pairs that must separate with the setting of the sun; the whole night long they call out to their separated mates.

chakor: ("trembling") the Indian partridge said to burst into song only when it beholds the full moon.

chakra: ("circle," "sphere," "discus") the spheres of energy that run along the spine and up to the brain, according to Yogic belief. There are six such spheres.

CHAKRADHAR: ("Discus-Holder") a name for Vishnu.

chandal: ("dog-eater," "cruel") one of the lowest castes, whose members dispose of all dead things, and also carry corpses to cremation grounds.

chatrik: ("charming") the cuckoo, which is said to live on raindrops alone, and therefore eagerly awaits the monsoon season.

CHITRA-GUPTA: ("Visible-Invisible") two scribes who record the deeds of human beings; they serve Yama, god of the dead.

DAMODAR: ("Tied Around the Middle") an epithet for Krishna. This refers to the practice of his stepmother (Yashodha) who tied him with a rope when he was especially mischievous.

DASRATHA: ("Ten Chariots") the father of the hero Ram Chandra. Also, JASRATH ("Splendid Chariot").

dervish: ("wanderer") a Muslim holy man, often dressed in black.

DEVA: ("Bright") God or divinity. Cf. the Latin *deus, divus*, and Greek *theos*.

DEVAKI: ("From the Gods") the mother of Krishna.

DHANVANTRI: ("Possessor of Wealth") the physician of the gods.

DHARAMRAJA: ("King of Justice") another name for Yama, god of the dead.

DHRUVA: ("Fixed") a great sage who for his piety was changed into the Pole Star by Vishnu, which never moves from its position.

dom: ("singer") low-caste musicians and cremation ground attendants, and probable ancestors of the Gypsies.

DRAUPADI: ("Daughter of Draupada") the collective wife of the five Pandava brothers, and heroine of the epic *The Mahabharata*.

DUSHASANA: ("Hard Counsel") one of a hundred sons of Dhrtarashtra, king of the Kauravas, the villains of *The Mahabharata*.

DURVASA: ("Ill-Clad") an evil-tempered sage, who cursed the Yadavas (Krishna's clan) to complete annihilation.

DURYODHANA: ("Hard in Battle") the eldest son of Dhrtarashtra.

DWARKA: ("High-Gated") the capital city of Krishna's later kingdom, situated west of Gujarat.

fakir: ("beggar") a wandering Muslim ascetic.

GANESHA: ("Lord of Hosts") the elephant-headed god of wealth and learning, son of Shiva and Parvati.

GANGES: ("Going") a sacred river said to flow from the hair of Shiva in the Himalayas.

GARUDA: ("Devourer") the eagle-faced man-bird that Vishnu rides. Garuda is the king of all the birds.

GAUTAMA: ("High-Worded") a sage whose wife Ahlaya was the lover of the god Indra.

GAYA: ("Booty," "Plunder") one of the holiest shrines in Hinduism, where grains are offered to the *Pitri* ("Forefathers"). Here also the Buddha received enlightenment.

GAYATRI: ("Song") the most sacred verse in *The Rig Veda*.

GITA GOVINDA: ("Song of Govinda," that is, Krishna) a song-cycle in Sanskrit written by Jayadeva, the famous twelfth-century poet; the work describes the erotic love between Radha and Krishna.

GOBIND: ("Binder of Cows") an epithet for Krishna. Also, GOVINDA.

GODAVARI: ("Cow-Giver") a river in eastern India.

GOKUL: ("Herd of Cows," "Cowshed") the village in Bindraban forest where Krishna was raised by his foster-parents, Yashodha and Nanda.

GOMTI: ("Cow-Feeder") a river in eastern India.

GOPAL: ("Cow-Nourisher") a name for Krishna.

GORAKH DATTA: ("Given by Gorakh," i.e., Shiva) the legendary founder of Nathism.

GOSAIN: ("Lord of Cows") originally a title for Brahmins, later applied to God. Also, GOSWAMI, SWAMI.

GREAT MOTHER: the female energy of Shiva, worshiped as Parvati, Durga, Bhavani, Oma, and Kali.

GURU: ("Great") the human guide that shows the path to inner enlightenment.

HANUMANA: ("Large-Jaws") the king of the monkeys and the helper of Ram Chandra in his fight against Ravana, the abductor of his wife.

HARI: ("Tawny") a name for Vishnu.

HARNAKHASA: ("Golden-Eyed") the father of the saint Prahlada. He was killed by Vishnu as Narsingh or man-lion, the god's fourth incarnation, for threatening his devotee Prahlada.

INDRA: ("Far-Shining," "Leader") the king of the gods, god of battle and of the sky, sender of rain. He rides the white elephant Airavata.

JAMUNA: ("Curved," "High-Banked") a sacred river that flows from the Himalayas and meets the Ganges.

JATS: a tribe of Indo-Aryans who settled in western parts of India and took up agriculture.

KALI: ("Black") a name of the Great Goddess in her destructive aspect.

KALIYA: ("Black One") a name of the giant snake who threatened the cows that came to drink at the river Jamuna; it was subdued by Krishna.

KAMDHENU: ("Cow of Desires") the magical cow, churned from the World Ocean, which fulfills all desires.

KAMLA: ("Lotus") another name for Lakshmi, the goddess of beauty and fortune and the wife of Vishnu.

KAMLAPATI: ("Lord of Kamla") a name for Vishnu.

KAMSA: ("Drinking-Cup") the king of the Bhojas and the cousin of Devaki, the mother of Krishna. He sought to kill the infant Krishna.

karma: ("act") The Hindu doctrine of actions (both religious and social) that lead to either good or bad results. This claim of cause and effect is the force that drives the transmigration of the soul, that determines the caste of a person, and that explains inequality and suffering in the world.

KAURAVAS: ("Doers") a clan of the Bharata tribe that fought against their cousins the Pandavas.

KAUSTUBHA: ("Support of the Earth") a magical gem churned from the World Ocean and worn on Vishnu's breast.

KEDARA: ("Dyked-Pond," "Irrigated Field") a shrine sacred to Shiva in the Himalayas.

KESHAVA: ("Long-Haired") a name for Shiva as a Yogi.

KESI: ("Hairy") a demon killed by Krishna.

KHAN: ("Lord") a Muslim name or title. Originally a title of Mongolian chieftains.

KHUDA: ("Self-Created") a Persian, hence Muslim, name for God.

KRATAR: ("Creator") God.

KRISHNA: ("Dark-Blue") one of Vishnu's incarnations. The major elements of Krishna's life are: his secret rearing in Gokul among cowherds; attempts on his life by his evil uncle Kamsa; his pranks as a child; his miracles; his sexual frolicking with the milkmaidens, especially with Radha; his defeat and killing of Kamsa; his aid of the Pandavas in their fight against the Kauravas; his revelation of his own divinity; his recitation of *The Bhagavad Gita*; and his death at the hands of a hunter.

kshatriya: ("protector," "keeper from harm") a member of the warrior caste, second only to Brahmins.

KUBERA: ("Deformed") the god of wealth, lord of the heavenly demi-gods (Yakshas and Guhyakas), and guardian of the north.

kundalini: ("twisted") the snakelike energy that lies coiled at the bottom of the spine; adept Yogis are said to drive this energy up to the brain and through the Tenth Door, where it unites with Shiva, inducing bliss and conferring salvation.

KURMA: ("Turtle") Vishnu's second incarnation. In the shape of a giant tortoise, Vishnu supported the mountain Mandara when the gods used it to churn the World Ocean in order to recover ambrosia that sustained them and kept them immortal.

KURUKSHETRA: ("Field of the Kauravas") the battlefield where the war between the Kauravas and the Pandavas was fought, as described in *The Mahabharata*.

LAKSHMI: ("Lucky," "Auspicious") wife of Vishnu, goddess of wealth, beauty, born from the World Ocean. Cf. Aphrodite.

LANKA: ("Rich") the island-kingdom of the demon Ravana who abducted Sita, Ram Chandra's wife. It was later identified with Ceylon or Sri Lanka.

lingam: ("phallus") the phallus of Shiva worshiped by his followers the Shaivites.

MADHO: (abbreviation of MADHAVA, "Killer of Madhu") an epithet for Krishna. Madhu was a demon.

MAHABHARATA: ("The Great Bharata") an epic poem that describes the dynastic struggles of two clans of the Bharata tribe (the Kauravas and the Pandavas). The poem consists of over ninety thousand stanzas and is the longest poem in the world.

MANSAROWAR: ("Lake Manasa," "Lake of Meditation") a holy lake, sacred to Shiva, in the Himalayas. Swans migrate there every winter and as such it represents the soul's final resting place.

mantra: ("measure," "spell," "charm") a word or verbal formula meant to evoke the inner presence of God. The literal meaning of *mantra* is "mental tool"; the root *man-* is etymologically related to the Latin *mens, mentis*, hence "mental."

MARKA: ("Great") a semidivine son of Brahma and the childhood teacher of the saint Prahlada.

MARKANDA: ("Winnower of Death") a great sage who lived for a long time; he is the Indian Methuselah.

MARWAR: desert region in central India.

MAYA: ("Magician") a goddess representing the world's unreality; she is often associated with the creative energy of the gods and is also an aspect of the Great Mother.

MONGOL: ("Brave Ones") a nomadic tribe from Mongolia who carved an empire stretching from China to Poland under their leader Ghengis Khan (1162–1227) and his descendants. In India the term came to designate a Muslim since the Turkic warriors that eventually invaded India had long converted to Islam. The terms *Mughal*(the dynasty that ruled northern India four hundred years before the British) or "Mogul" are derivations of *Mongol*.

MUKAND: ("Savior") an epithet for Krishna.

mullah: ("master") a Muslim cleric learned in theology and law.

MURARI: ("Slayer of Mura") a name for Krishna. Mura ("Violent") was one of the many demons that he slew.

NANDA: ("Joyous") Krishna's foster-father in Gokul; husband of Yashodha.

NARADA: ("Giving to Man") one of Brahma's sons and an accomplished sage; he was also the messenger of the gods, a heavenly musician, and a patron of singers. He was renowned for his sharp temper and loose tongue, and he was proud of his celibacy. To humble him, Vishnu changed him into a woman; as a woman he bore sixty sons to a king. Afterward he was changed again into a man. Cf. Teiresias.

NARAYANA: ("Born of Man") an ancient water deity, later identified with Vishnu.

NARSINGH: ("Man-Lion") Vishnu's fourth incarnation when he slew Harnakhasa.

nath: ("master") a follower of Nathism, the Yogic system of salvation.

NEJAYA: ("Triumphant") a sage of great antiquity about whom nothing is known.

nirvana: ("not being") existence that is beyond the passage of time into which the soul enters when it ceases its cycle of transmigration. Nirvana describes the state of redemption or moksha ("release") in the Hindu salvific process.

OM: ("Yes," "Amen") expresses the totality of creation and is the manifestation of the Word. It comes from Vedic ritual where it was used to affirm sacred incantations and praise. In this syllable is contained the completeness of God.

OMA: ("Light") one of the names of Parvati, the wife of Shiva.

PANDAVAS: ("Sons of Pandu") five brothers; adoptive sons of PANDU ("Blond," "Pale Yellow"), the king of Hastinapur. They were Yudhishtra, Bhima, and Arjuna, and the twins Nakula and Sahadeva. They were the rivals of the Kauravas for the throne and the heroes of *The Mahabharata*.

PARBRAHMA: ("Beyond Brahma") a name for the Absolute God.

PARMANANDA: ("Primal Bliss") a name for the Absolute God.

PARVATI: ("Daughter of the Mountain") the wife of Shiva.

PRABHU: ("Powerful," "Sovereign") an epithet for Krishna.

PRADYUMNA: ("Gift of Jamuna") Krishna's son killed before his very eyes during a riot of Yadava youths.

PRAHLADA: ("Joyous") a great sage, devoted to Vishnu for whom the god assumed his fourth incarnations (Narsingh) in order to protect his saint.

PURANAS: ("Old," "Ancient") the eighteen Hindu holy books that recount the deeds of the gods.

PURUSHOTAMA: ("Best of Beings") a name of Vishnu.

PUTANA: ("Stinking") a wet-nurse sent by Kamsa to kill the infant Krishna. She poisoned her nipples and went to nurse the baby. Krishna sucked out not only all her milk but her life as well. Before she died, she repented of her sin.

qalandar: ("recluse") a Muslim wandering ascetic.

qazi: ("judge") a Muslim religious judge or magistrate.

RADHA: ("Prosperity") the young milkmaiden whom Krishna loved in his youth. Their love is the subject of much bhakti literature. In later years, Krishna married Rukmini.

RAHU: ("Seizer") the demon that pursues the moon.

RAJA: ("King") sovereign, etymologically related to the Latin *rex*, Gothic *reiks*, Celtic *ri*.

RAM: ("Beautiful," "Charming") name of the Absolute God. Originally this name referred to RAM CHANDRA, who was an incarnation of Vishnu.

RAM CHANDRA: ("Beautiful Moon") the son of DASRATHA, and the hero of *The Ramayana*.

RAMAYANA: ("The Journey of Ram") an epic poem composed by the sage Valmiki, which tells the tale of Ram's efforts to recover his wife Sita who was abducted by Ravana, the king of Lanka. The poem has been called *The Iliad* of India.

RAVANA: ("Shrieker") the villain in *The Ramayana*.

SANAKA: ("Ancient") the first of Brahma's four mind-born sons. The other three were Sanandana, Sanatana, and Sanat Kumara. All four were renowned for their sagacity.

SANDA: ("Strong") one of Brahma's semidivine sons, and a teacher of Prahlada.

sant: ("holy") a reform movement within Hinduism whose members did not follow any dogma or doctrine but chose to worship God with personal ardor and ecstatic love.

SARANGDHAR: ("Holder of Sarang") a name for Vishnu. SARANG ("Speckled") is the name of Vishnu's bow.

SHASTRA: ("Treatise") six Hindu philosophical systems that outline various programs for salvation. Yoga is one such system.

sheikh: ("venerable old man") a Muslim spiritual leader and guide.

SHIVA: ("Auspicious") the God of cosmic creation and destruction.

SHUDRA: ("Servant") the lowest of the four Hindu castes.

SHYAMA: ("Dusky") one of Krishna's names.

SIDDHAS: ("Accomplished") semidivine beings who inhabit middle-air (the space between heaven and earth). They have great miraculous powers.

SIRAT: ("Bridge") the bridge that spans Hell and leads to heaven, according to Muslim belief. It is said to be as thin as a single strand of hair and as sharp as a sword. Only the righteous can walk across it to paradise; sinners fall into Hell.

SITA: ("Furrow") the wife of Ram Chandra, who was abducted by Ravana, and then rescued by her husband, as recounted in *The Ramayana*.

SMRITI: ("Remembered") twenty-seven collections of Hindu law and ceremony.

SRIRANG: ("Lakshmi's Lover") Vishnu as he is known in South India.

SUDAMA: ("Beautiful") Krishna's childhood friend to whom he gave many riches because of the constant love Sudama bore him.

UGARSAINA: ("Frightening Troop") the father of Kamsa, the evil king who wanted to kill Krishna. When Krishna defeated and killed Kamsa, he gave the kingdom to Ugarsaina.

UPANISHADS: ("Sitting Beneath") the mystical books that outline God's universality. There are said to be 108 of them.

vaishnava: ("Vishnu-ite") a follower of Vishnu.

vaishya: ("artisan") the third of the Aryan castes of farmers, artisans, and merchants.

VALMIKI: ("Penitent of the Ant-hill") the chandal whom Krishna fed after the battle of Kurukshetra to demonstrate that even a casteless man who is close to God is better than an inattentive Brahmin. The second instance of this name is the sage who composed *The Ramayana*.

VAMANA: ("Short," "Dwarf") Vishnu's fifth incarnation as a dwarf in which shape he rescued the universe from Bali.

VASUDEVA: ("Lord of Wealth") the father of Krishna.

VASUKI: ("Dweller") a great serpent whom the gods lashed about the Mandara Mountain, as a cord, in order to churn the World Ocean. Sometimes identified with SESHNAGA ("Six-headed Snake") the World serpent that lies coiled at the bottom of the earth. Cf. the Norse Midgard serpent JÓRMUNGANDR.

VEDAS: ("Wisdom") the four foundational Scriptures of Hinduism: *The Rig Veda* (hymns to be used during sacrifices), *The Sama Veda* (particular verses from *The Rig Veda* for liturgical use), *The Yajur Veda* (sacrificial formulas to be chanted during a sacrifice), and *The Atharva Veda* (magical spells and verse incantations).

VIBHISHANA: ("Frightening") Ravana's brother who fought against him, in support of Ram Chandra. After the defeat of Ravana, the kingdom of Lanka was given to Vibhishana.

VIDURA: ("Wise") a poor, low-caste man with whom Krishna stayed. Not to be confused with VIDURA who was a half-brother to Dhrtarashtra and an adviser to the Pandavas.

VISHNU: ("All-Pervasive") the god who sustains the world.

VYASA: ("Gatherer," "Compiler") the great sage who is said to have compiled the four *Vedas* and who composed *The Mahabharata*.

YADAVA: ("Descendants of Yadu") the clan to which Krishna belonged.

YAMA: ("Twin") the god of the dead and lord of the Underworld. Cf. the Latin *geminus*, and the French *jumeau*.

YASHODHA: ("Fame-Giver") the wife of Nanda and foster-mother of Krishna.

Yoga: ("yoke") a system of salvation based upon rigorous physical and mental discipline, which consists of yama (self-control), niyama (attentiveness), asana (bodily postures), pranayama (breath control), pratyahara (control of the senses), dharana (mind control), dhyana (meditation), and samadhi (intense meditation). There are four types of Yoga: Raja Yoga (royal Yoga) which deals with psychic and mental activities; it is deemed the highest form of Yoga; Mantra Yoga (Yoga of spells) is concerned exclusively with mastering magic; Laya Yoga (Yoga of dissolution) teaches trances and subconscious processes; and Hatha or Kundalini Yoga (Yoga of force, or yoga of the spiral) which enjoins physical training.

Yogi: ("doer of Yoga") one who practices Yoga and follows the teachings of Gorakh DATTA.

INDEX